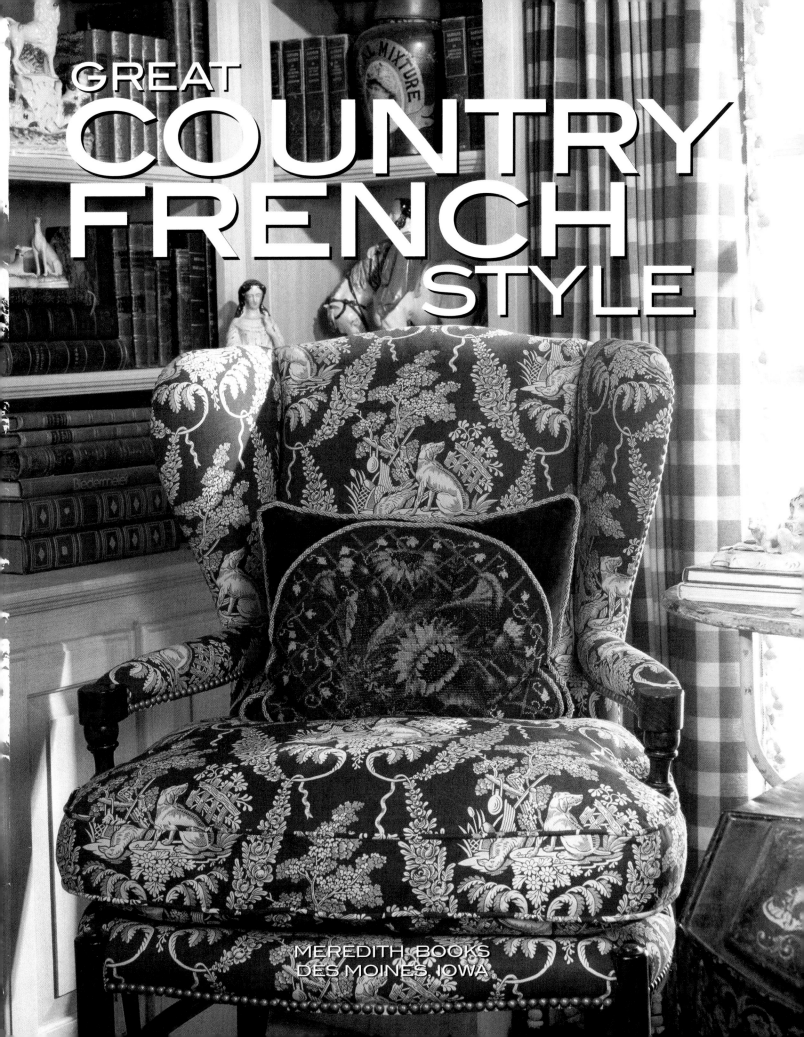

# GREAT COUNTRY FRENCH STYLE

MEREDITH BOOKS
DES MOINES, IOWA

*Great Country French Style*
Contributing Writer: Michele Keith
Contributing Editor: Wanda Ventling
Contributing Graphic Designer: Sundie Ruppert, Studio G
Assistant Art Director: Erin Burns
Copy Chief: Terri Fredrickson
Publishing Operations Manager: Karen Schirm
Senior Editor, Asset & Information Management: Phillip Morgan
Edit and Design Production Coordinator: Mary Lee Gavin
Editorial Assistant: Kaye Chabot
Book Production Managers: Pam Kvitne, Marjorie J. Schenkelberg,
    Rick von Holdt, Mark Weaver
Contributing Copy Editor: Nancy Evans
Contributing Proofreaders: Pam Elizian, Sue Fetters, Juliet Jacobs
Contributing Cover Photographer: Linda Hanselman
Contributing Indexer: Sharon Duffy

**Meredith® Books**
Executive Director, Editorial: Gregory H. Kayko
Executive Director, Design: Matt Strelecki
Managing Editor: Amy Tincher-Durik
Senior Editor/Group Manager: Vicki Leigh Ingham
Senior Associate Design Director: Mick Schnepf
Marketing Product Manager: Steve Rogers

Publisher and Editor in Chief: James D. Blume
Editorial Director: Linda Raglan Cunningham
Executive Director, Marketing: Steve Malone
Executive Director, New Business Development: Todd M. Davis
Executive Director, Sales: Ken Zagor
Director, Operations: George A. Susral
Director, Production: Douglas M. Johnston
Director, Marketing: Amy Nichols
Business Director: Jim Leonard

Vice President and General Manager: Douglas J. Guendel

**Meredith Publishing Group**
President: Jack Griffin
Executive Vice President: Bob Mate

**Meredith Corporation**
Chairman and Chief Executive Officer: William T. Kerr
President and Chief Operating Officer: Stephen M. Lacy

In Memoriam: E.T. Meredith III (1933-2003)

All of us at Meredith® Books are dedicated to providing you with information and ideas to enhance your home. We welcome your comments and suggestions. Write to us at: Meredith Books, Home Decorating and Design Editorial Department, 1716 Locust St., Des Moines, IA 50309-3023.

# TABLE OF CONTENTS

# INTRODUCTION

Mention country French, and most people envision a stone house with beamed ceilings and rooms filled with richly carved armoires and cozy sofas upholstered in toile de Jouy. One or two of those little iron chairs usually seen in Parisian public gardens might be pulled up to the hearth holding a stack of books or a pitcher of sunflowers.

Country French is all that and more. What makes its many interpretations so livable, and why country French continues to be among the most popular interior design motifs in America, is that it never forgets its past even while charging ahead into the future. And perhaps of even greater significance, homes created in this manner always reflect the occupants' personalities, which makes each house unique. A brilliant combination of the rustic with the refined, country French is as correct for a cottage as it is for a château.

Like all things related to French style, country French had its beginning in the late 1600s, when Louis XIV began his campaign to turn France into the capital of good taste. According to Joan DeJean, author of *The Essence of Style*, the first step, letting loose hundreds of swans onto the Seine to add a decorative note to the river, developed into dozens of programs to set people talking about the elegance of Paris and all that originated there. An extraordinary dandy—he wore diamonds as casually as we wear sneakers, even decorating his shoes with them—the Sun King legislated everything from the way stores sold merchandise to the refreshments served in cafes to the clothing people wore.

Most important to the king was the decoration of the official residence, the palace of Versailles. Louis and his ministers worked closely with scores of craftspeople. Whether glassblower, mirror maker, or rug weaver, those artisans whose mission was to beautify the huge rooms were given aid of every sort to help them produce the most glorious and upscale products. And the king made sure that there were markets for their goods not only in France but throughout Europe. By the early 18th century the French had acquired a monopoly on style and luxurious living.

While evolving over time to meet the needs of the middle class and their much simpler homes, the basics of country French decorating—proportion, balance, and fine craftsmanship—have never wavered. Add to this the importance the French put on the family, and you end up with a style that is above all pleasing to the eye and comfortable to live with.

In this book you'll see the entire gamut of country French designs realized in a variety of individual and interesting ways. Enjoy them all and become inspired to add a little country French to your life and surroundings.

COLOR IS KEY. PERENNIAL FAVORITES INCLUDE THE FRENCH FLAG'S BLUE, WHITE, AND RED; THE BOLD YELLOWS AND EARTHY BROWNS FOUND IN PROVENCE; THE BLUES OF THE OCEAN, SKY, AND FLOWERS ON THE CÔTE D'AZUR; AND THE MOSSY GREENS, PINKS, AND CREAMS OF COUNTRY FARMS AND MEADOWS.

PATTERNS THAT DOMINATE INCLUDE TOILE DE JOUY, WHICH ARE SINGLE-COLOR PICTORIAL SCENES, ESPECIALLY IN BLUE, RED, OR GREEN ON AN IVORY BACKGROUND; GINGHAMS, OVERSIZE CHECKS, OR PLAIDS OFTEN USED TOGETHER; WIDE AWNING STRIPES AND NARROW TICKING; AND TINY BOUQUETS AND ASIAN-INSPIRED BOUGHS LADEN WITH BLOSSOMS. ANIMAL PRINTS AND THE BEE MOTIF USED BY NAPOLEON ARE OFTEN SEEN AS ACCENTS.

**FABRICS** HEAVILY INFLUENCE THE LEVEL OF GRANDEUR IN A SPACE. FOR ELEGANT DRAPERIES AND UPHOLSTERY THERE ARE DAMASK, SILK, SATIN, AND TAFFETA. A MORE HOMESPUN FEEL RESULTS FROM COTTON, CHINTZ, AND MUSLIN. IN BETWEEN, VERSATILE LINEN, VOILE, AND TAPESTRIES CAN GO EITHER WAY. KEY TO THE COUNTRY FRENCH LOOK IS THE LAYERING OF COLORS, PATTERNS, AND TEXTURES, WHICH PROVIDES A DEPTH AND WARMTH UNOBTAINABLE BY OTHER MEANS.

**FURNITURE** RUNS THE GAMUT FROM THE GILDED TO THE NICKED AND CHIPPED. ARMOIRES CAN BE SIMPLE WOODEN AFFAIRS OR LAVISH WITH MARQUETRY. CHAIRS MAY BE NAIL-HEADED BERGÈRES CLOAKED IN SUEDE OR LADDERBACKS WITH RUSH SEATS. TABLES RANGE FROM THOSE WITH MARBLE TOPS AND IRON BASES, ONCE USED FOR ROLLING PASTRY DOUGH, TO INLAID MAHOGANY DESIGNS WORTH THEIR WEIGHT IN GOLD. MIXING AND MATCHING IS ENCOURAGED.

**FLOORS** ARE WIDE-PLANKED WOOD (EITHER PLAIN OR PAINTED), TERRA-COTTA, OR BRICK TO SUIT INFORMAL SPACES. PARQUET, TILES ARRANGED IN HERRINGBONE PATTERNS, AND MARBLE IN BLACK-AND-WHITE CHECKERBOARD CONFIGURATIONS ARE POPULAR FOR GRANDER HOMES. TIMEWORN ORIENTALS WORK WELL IN BOTH FANCY AND HUMBLE DWELLINGS, WHILE SISAL ADDS A CASUAL FEEL. SMALL NEEDLEPOINT AREA RUGS WARM THE HEARTH OR THE FLOOR BESIDE A BED.

**ACCESSORIES** ARE THE FINAL TOUCH THAT CAN TURN A NEARLY COUNTRY FRENCH LOOK INTO THE REAL THING. CHANDELIERS AND SCONCES ARE WONDERFUL WHETHER ORNATE AND DRIPPING WITH CRYSTALS OR COMPOSED OF A FEW IRON BRANCHES DECKED WITH STUBBY CANDLES. TÔLE LAMPSHADES AND CACHEPOTS ADD A GENUINE GALLIC NUANCE. PILLOWS COVERED WITH FRAGMENTS OF TAPESTRY AND EMBELLISHED WITH PASSEMENTERIE OR SLIPCOVERED IN PLAIN COTTON RAMP UP THE COMFORT QUOTIENT. COLLECTIONS AMASSED OVER THE YEARS ADD A DELIGHTFUL PERSONAL TOUCH, WHETHER THEY ARE EASY-TO-FIND LIMOGES BOXES OR RARE MAJOLICA EARTHENWARE. MIRRORS, PAINTINGS, PHOTOGRAPHY, AND SCULPTURE ALWAYS PLAY A ROLE IN THIS STYLE.

# 1 Redefined Elegance

# A French Fairy Tale

## Remodeling creates an interior to match the magical exterior of an old stone house.

**LEFT** AN ANTIQUE CHAIR, INTRICATELY CARVED AND PROUD OF ITS PEELING ORIGINAL PAINT, IS ONE OF MANY PIECES IN THE GUEST BEDROOM DRESSED IN RED-AND-WHITE TOILE.

**OPPOSITE** BRINGING TO MIND AN ANCIENT CASTLE DOOR, VINTAGE CARVED MOLDINGS FRAME THE STONE-FLOORED FOYER THAT LEADS TO THE MASTER BEDROOM.

10

Perched on three lush acres in Montecito, California, the gabled house "looked like something straight out of a fairy tale," says C. Lee Kirch. It was a veritable dream come true—until she walked inside.

"My heart sank," says Lee, but not for long. A designer with two stores and an interior decorating business, she had both the knowledge and the energy to take the required action—in this case, a total gutting and starting over. "The floors came out. The walls came out." It became such an enormous undertaking that she hired craftsman and contractor Michael Noonan to help. (CONTINUED ON PAGE 17)

**LEFT** THE LIVING ROOM MIXES ANTIQUES, SUCH AS THE FRENCH PILLOW COVERS AND 1930S NEEDLEPOINT RUG, WITH NEW PIECES LIKE THE CARVED MARBLE FIREPLACE, CUSTOM SOFA, AND COFFEE TABLE.

**PAGE 14** LIKE A VAST IMPRESSIONIST PAINTING, THE EXPANSIVE VIEW OF THE TERRACED GARDENS BECOMES A PART OF THE INTERIOR DESIGN SCHEME.

**PAGE 15** A RICHLY GLAZED MAJOLICA CACHEPOT, PART OF LEE'S EXTENSIVE COLLECTION, HOLDS A BOUQUET OF RANUNCULUS.

**OPPOSITE** A 19TH-CENTURY FRENCH CANAPÉ, OR SETTEE, FOUND IN PARIS WAS COMPLETELY REBUILT AND UPHOLSTERED IN BELGIAN LINEN. ITS GENTLE CURVES PLAY WELL ALONGSIDE THE TABLE AND ROMANTICALLY SHADED LAMP WITH ITS LEAF-EMBELLISHED, BRASS BASE.

**RIGHT** FLOWERS BLOOM IN THE ENTRY HALL WITH THE TAPESTRY-UPHOLSTERED CHAIRS, A SECRÉTAIRE LAVISHLY CRAFTED WITH MARQUETRY, AND A FANCIFULLY CARVED, CIRCA-1870 OAK TABLE.

Right away ceilings were raised to reflect the gabled roofline. Old barn wood became beams and walls, French limestone and antique bricks were imported for flooring, and exquisite carved moldings were located to frame doorways.

Filling the many rooms with furniture, fixtures, and decorative objets d'art became Lee's number-one priority. Traveling the French countryside, she picked up chairs, armoires, and a bureau. "I went to see antiques dealers who sell to other dealers," she says. "I was in a lot of old barns with a lot of bees flying around me." Ironically, it was through dealers in the United States that she acquired furnishings from the estate of the legendary Pierre Deux. To the antiques she added reproduction and handcrafted pieces upholstered in a romantic array of rich toiles, florals, and prints.

**LEFT** ALTHOUGH WALLED IN STONE AND FLOORED IN BRICK, THE DINING ROOM HAS A COZY AMBIENCE OWING TO THE INFUSION OF NATURAL LIGHT FLOWING IN FROM THE FRENCH DOORS AND THE ROOM'S MANY SCONCES AND LAMPS. THE ANTIQUE TABLE IS SURROUNDED BY CUSTOM-MADE RUSH-SEATED CHAIRS.

**OPPOSITE** THE STONE HALLWAY LEADING TO THE DINING ROOM WAS CONSTRUCTED WITH ARCHED COLUMNS EVOCATIVE OF A CENTURIES-OLD CHÂTEAU. GLEAMING PIECES, CAREFULLY POSITIONED FOR HANDY STORAGE AND SERVING, ADD A HOMEY NOTE.

In the "wine-dining room," as she's named it (because of its resemblance to a wine cellar in a grand château), are an 18th-century French carved-wood fireplace and a bodacious wood chandelier. Built-in niches coddle favorite vintages and a found store counter acts as a buffet. For more casual meals, the breakfast room just off the old-world kitchen features a table from 1700s France covered in a roughly woven yellow cloth with off-center red stripes that gently tie in with the patterned seat cushions.

**OPPOSITE** ALMOST LIKE BEING IN THE GARDEN, THE BREAKFAST ROOM HAS A COUNTRY SPIRIT WITH ITS SIMPLE SEATING ARRANGEMENT, MOTTLED STONE-TILED FLOOR, AND SUNNY DECOR.

**LEFT** LAYERED WITH A MULTITUDE OF TEXTURES AND FINISHES—SATINY WOOD AND COOL MARBLE, ROUGH BRICK AND NICKED WOOD—THE HIGHLY ORGANIZED KITCHEN IS AN EFFICIENT PLACE TO PREPARE MEALS AND A RELAXING SPOT FOR FRIENDS TO GATHER.

**ABOVE** REACHING NEARLY TO THE SOARING CEILING, THE IMMENSE ARMOIRE HOLDS A CACHE OF DECORATIVE CROCKERY FOUND THROUGHOUT EUROPE. THE SHELVED UPPER HALF IS LINED WITH A TOILE THAT COMPLEMENTS THE ROOM'S COLOR SCHEME.

Arranged throughout the house are charming oil paintings, majolica and earthenware pots, sun-faded rugs, and always lots of flowers. While no longer the owner, Lee is on call for design advice to the current residents. "My creative side enjoys every space in this home, and hearing the owners express their love for it makes the commitment I had to this project completely worthwhile."

**LEFT** THE MASTER BATH IS A VERITABLE RETREAT. MUTED COLORS SOOTHE, BUILT-IN FLOOR-TO-CEILING STORAGE UNITS KEEP CLUTTER TO AN ABSOLUTE MINIMUM, AND THE COMFORTABLY OVERSIZE TUB HAS A BREATHTAKING VIEW OF THE GARDEN.

**OPPOSITE** ELEGANTLY RUSTIC, THE MASTER BEDROOM COMBINES A WOOD FLOOR AND EXPOSED BEAMS WITH FINE ANTIQUES PULLED TOGETHER BY A DELICATE ARRAY OF TEXTURES AND PATTERNS. THE ARCHED MIRROR, DATING FROM 18TH-CENTURY FRANCE, LENDS A GLAMOROUS NOTE WITH ITS HIGH-RELIEF ORNAMENTATION.

Filled with natural sunlight, the master bath and bedroom exhibit the same exquisite attention to detail. Spa-like in its amenities, the bath is cozy with custom furniture and shaded sconces, while the bedroom, which overlooks a garden, is all curves and femininity with beautifully carved woodwork and passementerie-embellished pillows. It's definitely fit for a queen—or at least, a fairy princess.

THE UNUSUAL ADDITIONS
OF GRAY TO THE RED-
AND-WHITE COLOR
SCHEME AND OF STRIPES
TO THE TOILE AND
FLOWERED PATTERNS
CREATE A SOPHISTICATED
GUEST ROOM. THE
MUSTARD YELLOW
BUREAU DATES FROM
EARLY 19TH-CENTURY
FRANCE.

# New Take on Tradition

## Grandeur has a cozy edge in historic New Orleans.

LEFT A GOLD-EMBELLISHED CENTERPIECE AND LIMOGES CHINA ADD TO THE GLOW OF THE DINING ROOM, WHICH SHIMMERS UNDER A GOLD-LEAF CEILING.

OPPOSITE BACKED BY AN 18TH-CENTURY MURAL, THE ANTIQUE FRENCH WALNUT DESK WITH BLACK LEATHER TOP AND GILT HIGHLIGHTS IS PAIRED WITH A LOUIS XVI CHAIR.

Awash with sunlight,
the living room takes
on a carefree attitude.
A pair of Louis XV
chairs upholstered
in melon and green
stripes flanks the
fireplace. The canapé
dates from the time of
Louis XVI.

In the tradition of Marie Antoinette's country cottage, Le Petit Trianon, Vicky and Lewis McHenry's circa-1900 house in New Orleans, combines luxurious elegance with welcoming warmth. Restored to its original beauty during a laborious, 18-month process that included replacing the wood floors, moldings, and fireplace facades removed by previous owners, the residence now fairly glows.

Tutored from childhood by his knowledgeable mother, Lewis became an astute judge of antiques and began buying rare pieces while a student at Oxford University. "Because I'd grown up with a lot of old, mostly French furniture," he says, "I knew what was good and what wasn't. When I came back to New Orleans, it just made all the sense in the world. You want to have a style that's in keeping with the house." With Vicky, who is equally involved in their home's decor, he continues to educate himself and their two daughters and to enjoy the treasures they have amassed over the years.

**LEFT** LIGHTING UP A
CORNER OF THE LIVING
ROOM IS A LATE-17TH-
CENTURY DRAWING OF
AN IMAGE FROM THE
SISTINE CHAPEL DONE
ON PARCHMENT. THE
FRAME'S GILT DETAILING
IS UNDERSCORED BY THE
ACCESSORIES DISPLAYED
ON THE ANTIQUE TABLE
BENEATH.

**OPPOSITE** THE
FIREPLACE WAS
UPGRADED BY THE
MCHENRYS WITH AN
ANTIQUE MARBLE
MANTEL; ITS GILT
ORNAMENTATION
ANCHORS THE GILDED
FRENCH MIRROR ABOVE.

All the furnishings and artwork were in place when the McHenrys brought in esteemed interior designer Gerrie Bremermann to, as she describes it, "help Lewis to fluff it up a little more." For him, she says, "you can't get too dressy or too grand." Gerrie's job centered on formulating the primary color scheme, window treatments, upholstery, and the occasional addition of a piece of furniture.

Setting the stage for the palette of orange, melon, and gold, Gerrie designed fringe-embellished, bittersweet-hue silk drapes and hung them on simple gold rods in the living room. "When you walk in," says Lewis, "it's striking, it's warm, it's welcoming, it's dynamic." While much of the furniture and accessories is gilded and museum quality (the early-19th-century mantel clock, for example, has been cataloged by The Smithsonian Institution), the room is anything but intimidating. Enveloped in warm colors, with sunlight pouring in and familial touches such as pillows, photos, and flowers scattered about, it beckons visitors to enter and sink gently into the down-filled, damask-covered canapé or to draw up to the hearth one of the sweetly striped fauteuils.

**OPPOSITE** THE RENOVATION CREATED BETTER FLOW BETWEEN LIVING AND DINING ROOMS AND MADE BOTH AREAS APPEAR LARGER, AS DID THE SIMPLE COLUMN DETAILING AND IDENTICAL COLOR SCHEMES.

**LEFT** THE GOLD-LEAF CEILING BRINGS OUT THE BAS RELIEF ON THE CUPBOARD DOORS AND REPEATS IN THE GOLD FLATWARE AND TABLETOP ACCESSORIES USED FOR ENTERTAINING.

Other areas in the residence, such as the dining room with its Louis Philippe chairs, gold-leaf ceiling, and French crystal chandelier, are equally high caliber, decorated with rare antiques. But there are also rooms such as the solarium and den that are simpler, defined by relatively plain wood pieces and crisp cottons in florals and plaids. Connecting them are the color scheme and an exquisite attention to detail.

Haute design yet comfortably down to earth, the McHenry home illustrates how one can live with the finest antiques in a carefree, natural way.

**ABOVE** Inherited from Lewis's great-grandmother, the Mallard bed dates from before the Civil War. The tester, or canopy, displays checks underneath and a floral pattern above.

**OPPOSITE** The solarium off the master bedroom was cocooned in stripes to hide structural imperfections. The antebellum daybed and tea table are family heirlooms.

**PAGES 36–37** The sofa's large-scale floral fabric was worn out by the McHenrys, says Gerrie, but it was such a favorite, "We put it right back on again."

# Old Is New Again

A NEW HOME IS BUILT
IN CHICAGO TO LOOK,
FEEL—AND SOUND—OLD.

**LEFT** TO GIVE A
HISTORICAL LOOK TO
THE GARAGE, A BRONZE
FINISH WAS PUT ON
THE OVERHANG AND A
VERDIGRIS FINISH ON THE
COACH LIGHT.

**OPPOSITE** COMPLETE
WITH A BRONZE-CAST
DOOR KNOCKER, MAIL
SLOT, AND LOCK SET, THE
FRONT DOOR IS WARM
AND INVITING.

**OPPOSITE** THE NEW HOUSE IS ROOFED WITH 100-YEAR-OLD SLATE AND DESIGNED WITHOUT GUTTERS, SOFFITS, OR MOLDINGS FOR A MORE HISTORICALLY ACCURATE APPEARANCE.

**RIGHT** BEDECKED WITH FLOWERS, THE GARAGE WAS DESIGNED IN EXACTLY THE SAME STYLE AS THE HOUSE, RIGHT DOWN TO THE DORMER WINDOWS AND SLATE ROOF.

"The French do everything right," says Tim Thompson. That includes interior design. French rooms done well always make you feel so comfortable, says this Chicago-based general contractor. So when he and his wife, Carol, decided to build a new house, they naturally took as their inspiration the centuries-old cottages they had seen in France.

On the exterior, the new house boasts a multitude of traditional French features, including dormers, multipane windows, an arched front entrance, and hand-carved shutters. For an authentic look, the hipped roof is covered with hand-chipped slate salvaged from a 100-year-old house, and the walls are cement-colored stucco that changes from light pink to dark gray, brown, or white depending on the time and season.

Approaching the front of the house, visitors encounter an architectural trick Tim calls "compression and release." Small windows give the impression that it will be dark inside, while the low roofline makes visitors think they'll have to stoop to enter. But surprise! Once inside, guests are "released" into a light-filled space with ceilings that soar as high as 12 feet in places and marvelous banks of French doors and windows. "It's like this is a 100-year-old house that has been completely remodeled," says architect Michael Abraham, who worked on the project with fellow architect Michael Culligan. (CONTINUED ON PAGE 46)

**OPPOSITE** TIM SELECTED EACH STONE AND DESIGNED THE FOUR SWOOPING LINES ABOVE THE ENTRANCE TO EMPHASIZE THE DOOR'S ARCH. AN ACID WASH GAVE THE STONES AN AGED APPEARANCE.

**ABOVE** A HUMMINGBIRD EMBELLISHES THE CAST-BRONZE KNOB ON THE FRONT DOOR.

**PAGES 44–45** COMBINING ROUGH WITH SMOOTH, GLAMOROUS WITH RUSTIC, AND NEW WITH OLD, THE DINING ROOM'S DECOR IS SOPHISTICATED, SPARE, AND ELEGANT.

Keen on incorporating details taken from old French manses, Tim built a stucco-and-stone fireplace in the living room, used exposed pine beams to add structural support for the raised ceilings, and had the wide-plank hickory floors hand-scraped to distress them sufficiently for the look he was after. Such details as the antique-style 24-inch hinges on the bedroom door not only look old, they sound old—rattling when they're shut, just as Tim wanted.

Furnished with just enough curves to suggest your favorite period of Louis, the look is simple and inviting. With rafts of bookshelves and patterned area rugs anchoring conversation groups, formality is sensed but never overdone.

**ABOVE** LOOKING LIKE A SALVAGED PIECE FROM AN OLD FRENCH CHÂTEAU, THE STONE-AND-STUCCO FIREPLACE WAS INSPIRED BY MODERN MASTER FRANK LLOYD WRIGHT'S FALLINGWATER HOUSE.

**OPPOSITE** WALLED WITH FRENCH DOORS, THE LIVING ROOM HAS CEILINGS THAT RISE TO 12 FEET IN THE CENTER OF THE ROOM. THE BEAMS GIVE THE ROOM A COUNTRY EDGE.

**OPPOSITE** THE MATERIALS USED FOR THE KITCHEN APPROPRIATELY REFLECT BOTH HOT AND COLD—WOOD AND STONE, MARBLE AND STAINLESS STEEL. SMALL PENDANT LIGHTS MIMIC THE SHAPE OF THE STOVE'S HOOD.

**RIGHT** A CORNER OF THE HOME'S 46-FOOT-LONG INTERIOR STONE WALL IS SEEN AT THE END OF THE HALL LEADING FROM THE KITCHEN.

When it came to the kitchen, Abraham says, "In a 300-year-old European house, the kitchen has been redone 15 times. Europeans are known for their slick, streamlined kitchens contrasted against old interiors." His version pairs hand-crafted white-birch cabinetry, stone floors, and mahogany countertops with stainless-steel appliances, a glass-fronted refrigerator, and contemporary pendant lights.

A house for the ages, it represents Tim's design philosophy: "New things should look authentic and should appeal to all your senses. When you see them and touch them, there should be no tip-off that they're new."

NEARLY ALL WINDOWS,
THE SUNROOM FEATURES
100-YEAR-OLD SASHES
FITTED WITH NEW, WAVY-
PATTERNED GLASS. "FROM
THE INSIDE OUT," SAYS TIM,
"IT LOOKS LIKE A FRENCH
IMPRESSIONIST PAINTING."

# Haute Country Living

The feeling of forever is established in a new North Carolina home.

**LEFT** Used for the homeowners' frequent entertaining, etched glassware adds a sublime sparkle to every dinner party.

**OPPOSITE** Checkerboard squares, flowers, and stripes create an elegant foyer.

The impression of permanence resounds in French homes. Even within renovated interiors one senses that the original soul of the house still lingers. This was the feeling Cathy and Scott Bortz wanted for their new home in Charlotte.

Built to look on the outside as though it has graced the established neighborhood for generations, every room inside was carefully calculated as well, with equal attention to comfort and beauty. The easy, lived-in look encourages guests to enjoy themselves, prop up their feet, or make a cozy nest of pillows on the sofa.

(CONTINUED ON PAGE 58)

**OPPOSITE** A PICTURE OF PERFECT SYMMETRY, THE SOARING FOYER SHOWS OFF A REPRODUCTION TRUMEAU MIRROR, CHAIRS FROM THE 1840S, A REGENCY CHEST, AND A FEW OF CATHY'S FRENCH WATERCOLORS.

**LEFT** A SYMMETRICAL FACADE, HIPPED ROOF, DORMERS, AND SHUTTERS GIVE THIS NEW HOUSE A CLASSIC LOOK.

**PAGES 56–57** DEEP BULLION FRINGE OVER THE SOFA SKIRT AND A SCALLOPED LINE OF NAILHEADS ON THE OTTOMAN ADD EUROPEAN FLAIR TO SIMPLE, COMFORTABLE PIECES.

The magician who made it happen was Mark Phelps of Circa Interiors, who shares Cathy's love of French antiques. His traditional, tailored approach was perfect for the job, as was his inclination toward simple yet luxurious textiles and unusual ways with wallpaper and paint. By starting simply and adding uncommon touches, he created a highly personal abode for the family that conveys the aura of a refined French country home yet also delivers the modern efficiency of a thoroughly American one.

Entering the foyer, where you might expect a timeworn tapestry on a marble floor, visitors are instead greeted by a painted checkerboard of large black and white squares and walls papered with a sunny yellow, tone-on-tone stripe. The wall's cheerful color was carried into the living and dining rooms, creating a sense of place as well as unity.

(CONTINUED ON PAGE 63)

**OPPOSITE** CANED CHAIRS FROM 1820S FRANCE MIX WITH NEWER PIECES IN THE DINING ROOM.

**PAGES 60–61** LAYERING PATTERNS AND TEXTURES SETS UP A COUNTRY-CITY VIBE IN THE FAMILY ROOM. BAMBOO SHADES CONTRAST WITH FORMAL, FRINGED DRAPERIES; SPARKLING GILT FRAMES HIGHLIGHT SIMPLE WOODWORK; AND SOPHISTICATED LEOPARD SETS OFF DOWN-HOME CHECKS.

**OPPOSITE** CHINESE LAMPS REFLECT THE PASSION OF 19TH-CENTURY FRANCE FOR ALL THINGS ORIENTAL.

**RIGHT** THE TABLE LAMP WAS MADE FROM AN OLD CHINESE TEA CANISTER. PIECES FROM CATHY'S COLLECTION OF MAJOLICA TOP THE BUREAU.

Although the dining room is the most formal space in the house, its pastiche of fabrics, textures, and prints is just enough to provide a whiff of fresh country air. Playing off the classicism of the highly polished table are eight caned fruitwood chairs crafted in 1820s France, each cushioned with a picnic stripe of pink, green, and yellow. To the side, providing an inviting place to sip an after-dinner *digestif,* is a mid-19th-century French settee upholstered in a flowering vine print. And sparkling above, a simple chandelier hangs, adorned by a single strand of crystals.

In the family room checks, leopard print, and needlepoint add a bit of a rustic note so that the selection of fine French antiques looks perfectly at ease within the sea of soft yellow walls and sofas. In the master bedroom formal taffeta draperies contrast with the carved wooden bed, and nailhead trim balances softly sculpted bergères. A tour de force of country living, this is a home that will welcome many generations yet to come.

**ABOVE** OPENING ONTO A PRIVATE TERRACE, THIS COZY CORNER OF CATHY AND SCOTT'S MASTER BEDROOM PROVIDES A TRANQUIL RESPITE FROM THE LIVELY ANTICS OF THEIR FOUR CHILDREN.

**OPPOSITE** FLOODED WITH SUNLIGHT FROM SEVERAL FLOOR-TO-CEILING WINDOWS, THE SIMPLY FURNISHED MASTER BEDROOM HINTS AT OPULENCE WITH THE CRYSTAL CHANDELIER, LUXURIOUS TAFFETA CURTAINS, AND CREAMY WALL-TO-WALL CARPETING.

CARVED FRENCH CHAIRS FROM THE 1840S COVERED IN HERRINGBONE LINEN FLANK A PEMBROKE TABLE. THE JUXTAPOSITION OF CURVED AND STRAIGHT LINES KEEPS THE ROOM BALANCED IN MOOD— NEITHER TOO FUSSY NOR TOO SEVERE. WITH THE TABLE OPEN, THE CORNER CAN BE USED FOR QUIET DINNERS FOR TWO.

# Simply
# Grand

HOME TO TWO ANTIQUARIANS,
A NEW ORLEANS COTTAGE
IS FILLED WITH EUROPEAN
RARITIES AS WELL AS FLEA
MARKET FINDS.

**LEFT** AN ANTIQUE SILVER
CUP HOLDS FRESH ROSES.

**OPPOSITE** A FRENCH
DIRECTOIRE ARMCHAIR
AND A LOUIS XVI GILDED
OTTOMAN DRAW UP TO
AN ENGLISH SOFA TABLE
THAT DATES TO ABOUT
1810.

W

"We're in the aesthetic, spiritual, entertainment, and business heart of the Big Easy," says Jimmy Schneider who lives in the fabled Vieux Carré with wife Roslyn, not far from where he grew up. Surviving the devastation of Hurricane Katrina, their 1890 Louisiana cypress cottage is a quiet respite from the activity of the area. Set in a lush garden, it's a tranquil home that they've decorated with "fine 18th-century antiques as well as pieces prized more for their decoration than their age," says Jimmy. "I love antiques for the artistry employed in their creation and especially for their patina—the colors as they age, all the nicks and scratches, the satiny feel of old wood, used lovingly for decades." (CONTINUED ON PAGE 74)

**OPPOSITE** WITH ITS AIRY CANE BACK AND STRIPED CUSHION, THE CIRCA-1800 LOUIS XVI-STYLE SETTEE SUITS THE MIX OF FORMAL AND INFORMAL LIVING ROOM FURNISHINGS.

**OPPOSITE** A MATCHED SET OF LOUIS XV BERGÈRES WITH PAINTED FRAMES AND BLUSH DAMASK UPHOLSTERY ANCHORS THE SEATING GROUP IN THE LIVING ROOM. A CIRCA-1830 FRENCH GILDED MIRROR HANGS ABOVE THE HOME'S ORIGINAL MARBLE FIREPLACE.

**LEFT** A BEAUTIFULLY CONSERVED 19TH-CENTURY FRENCH TÔLE LAMP SHEDS LIGHT ON A LATE-18TH-CENTURY WALNUT LOUIS XV SIDE TABLE.

The furniture, the majority of it purchased while shopping for the couple's highly respected Uptowner Antiques shop, has been positioned into inviting groupings that encourage conversation or quiet dreaming. Ensconced in sunny rooms carpeted with faded antique Orientals, the upholstery on such pieces as the 1780 French bergères and Swedish beech-wood banquette designed à la Louis XV ranges from a soft peach damask to a fun red-and-white check. The effect is a leisurely formality.

Prized selections plucked from their shop include a late-18th-century French *secrétaire abbatant*, or writing desk, and a Louis XVI gilded ottoman. Throughout are marvelous paintings, chandeliers, and painted-and-carved mirrors that increase the drama of the soaring 12-foot ceilings.

AN 1810 ITALIAN MIRROR AND A LOUIS XVI WALNUT BUREAU HOLD COURT BETWEEN TWO FRENCH DOORS IN THE SITTING ROOM. THE EMPIRE CHAIR ON THE LEFT OF THE BUREAU IS UPHOLSTERED IN FABRIC EMBROIDERED WITH NAPOLEON'S BEE INSIGNIA. THE PROVENÇAL CHAIR ON THE RIGHT, DATING FROM THE 19TH CENTURY, IS UPHOLSTERED IN THAT REGION'S TYPICAL RED-AND-WHITE CHECK.

LEFT A QUEEN ANNE-STYLE FRUITWOOD BUFFET FROM THE 1790S IS A REGAL STORAGE UNIT FOR THE DINING ROOM'S NAPERY, SILVERWARE, AND OTHER ITEMS FOR ENTERTAINING.

OPPOSITE IN THE DINING ROOM, MID-19TH-CENTURY LOUIS XV-STYLE PAINTED CHAIRS RING A GLEAMING ANTIQUE DINING TABLE THAT STANDS ON DAINTY CASTERS. LIGHT SPARKLES FROM THE CRYSTAL-LADEN CHANDELIER AND REFLECTS OFF THE ORNATE GOLD-LEAF ITALIAN MIRROR AND ITALIAN CANDLESTICKS, BOTH FROM THE 18TH CENTURY.

Key to incorporating their personalities and giving an authentic feel to the house is the Schneiders' discriminating use of accessories. Like the French of the 1800s who were intrigued by everything coming out of China, they've added touches of Orientalia by way of lamps and porcelains. From the same period, tôle lamps enhance the glow of handrubbed fruitwood and walnut tables, while rare items such as the French plaster relief from the late 18th century hanging in the master bath add texture to painted walls.

**OPPOSITE** In the master bedroom a bergère from 1800, clad in vintage chenille, sits next to the French doors that open onto the garden. At the foot of the bed is a reproduction 18th-century walnut bench from Provence.

**ABOVE** Adding nuance to the master bath, a late-18th-century French plaster relief found at the New Orleans flea market hangs above a 19th-century American marble-top gilded shelf.

**RIGHT** Highlighting the master suite's 12-foot ceilings is an 18th-century trumeau mirror topped by a grisaille painting.

Bringing nature inside is a typical French design trick used to greatest effect in cities. The Schneiders have their own beautifully landscaped garden on the property, so filling gleaming silver pitchers and crystal vases with blooms they cut themselves adds a fresh touch of the outdoors to each room of their museum-quality house.

"It's fun being in the Quarter," says Roslyn. "As Jimmy says frequently, it's our retirement village—everything you need is right here within walking distance: shops, grocery stores, churches, a night on the town." And with three grown children frequently visiting, one can be certain that generations of Schneiders to come will feel the same way.

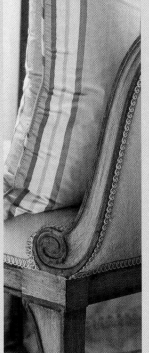

# 2 Broad Strokes of Color

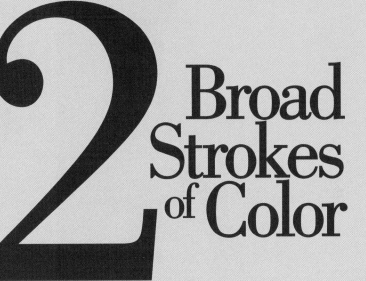

# Prints of Passion

RESTRAINED ABANDON
WHEN MIXING PATTERNS
AND TONES CREATES A
HOUSE UNLIKE ANY OTHER.

**LEFT** AN UNUSUAL AND HIGHLY COLLECTIBLE MAJOLICA CHEESE DOME IN THE SHAPE OF A STRAW HAT PERCHES ATOP A STACK OF BOOKS ON A LOUIS XVI CHAIR.

**OPPOSITE** ONE OF A PAIR, THE LAVISHLY BEADED PILLOW COVER WAS RECYCLED FROM A VICTORIAN TEA COZY.

**OPPOSITE** A Scottish painting from the 19th century and the Regency-style beechwood table with an uncommon fabric top highlight this corner of the library.

**RIGHT** Dating from the 1800s, the bust of a blackamoor market vendor stands out among many rare finds in this treasure-laden corner of the house.

**PAGES 86–87** A massive Chinese tea tin and a French cafe table holding a tôle cachepot, a lamp made from a Staffordshire figurine, and other objets d'art are tucked between two provincial-style wing chairs in the library-cum-sitting room.

Charles Faudree, one of the country's top authorities on decorating in the French country style, describes his favorite look this way: "French country is easy to love and easy to live with. It combines the rustic and the refined for a look that's both casual and elegant."

This home illustrates his celebrated modus operandi—a deliciously delirious mixture of flowered, checked, and toile fabrics; leopard and Oriental rugs; and rustic wood furniture straight from a provincial farmhouse placed side by side with pieces from the time of Louis XV. Accented top to bottom with artwork, statues, plates, and pillows, they aptly illustrate his philosophy that "too much is never enough." In the hands of a lesser talent, it would be overkill. With Charles's expert eye, it works beautifully. (CONTINUED ON PAGE 88)

PROVING CHARLES'S THEORY THAT WITH ORDER, EVEN LARGE COLLECTIONS OF DIVERSE OBJECTS CAN WORK IN A ROOM ARE THE MANY ITEMS ON AND AROUND THE BUFFET, INCLUDING THE BLUE-AND-WHITE EXPORT PORCELAIN, CONCRETE FLORAL BASKETS, AND TALL, GINGHAM-SHADED LAMPS.

"The secret is in the mix," he says. "The most interesting interiors mix influences and inspiration, old and new. It's the mix that helps a designer and a homeowner to personalize a space and make it truly one of a kind." To give each room a bit of a surprise, he often upholsters fancifully carved chairs with simple linen or juxtaposes reproductions with fine antiques. "Pairing unexpected elements is very French," he explains. (CONTINUED ON PAGE 93)

# PRINTS OF PASSION

**RIGHT** The kitchen cupboard's spare silhouette and country-check lining are the perfect foil for a display of decorated export porcelain.

**OPPOSITE** Bringing a bit of the outdoors in is a miniature wheelbarrow planted with French tulips and ivy. The wheelbarrow also adds to the mix of textures, which include marble, wood, and china.

**OPPOSITE** AMONG THE
DINING ROOM'S "INSTANT
ANCESTORS," AS CHARLES
CALLS ANTIQUES,
ARE THE VICTORIAN
TRANSFERWARE PIECES
DISPLAYED ON THE
WALLS, IN A FRENCH
OAK SIDEBOARD
DISTINGUISHED BY AN
OPEN CENTER, AND ON
THE TABLE.

**RIGHT** WHILE ACCENTED
WITH STRIPES, CHECKS,
AND FLORALS, THE
PREDOMINANT THEME
IN THE DINING ROOM IS
RED-AND-WHITE TOILE
AND BLUE-AND-WHITE
PORCELAIN.

When it comes to color, Charles leans toward red. Providing instant impact, red is particularly inviting in dens and bedrooms and is especially appealing when used in conjunction with those other colors of the French flag, blue and white. But even when he does up a room in neutrals, his signature focal point keeps it exciting. "Just one distinctive piece of furniture, such as an armoire or a chest or a great accessory like a grand mirror or painting, will make the rest of the room seem more important." Presenting the point nicely is the oil painting of a genteel lady in the dining room. Centered on the toile-covered wall, she brings a sense of order to the multitude of patterns around her, which in turn dramatizes the entire space.

And one needn't pay a king's ransom for such dramatic treasures, he counsels. "You can get the look without the 17th-century armoire. Painted furniture is really beautiful, so in vogue, and often quite reasonable in comparison to pricey antiques. The key is finding a piece you really love and want to live with forever."

Simple or sumptuous, the secret to French country's enduring appeal is its timelessness. "French country interiors are known for being warm and welcoming," says Charles. "It's a look that never goes out of style."

**ABOVE** AN ENGLISH REGENCY MIRROR HANGS ABOVE A FRENCH FRUITWOOD DESK.

**OPPOSITE** A PAINTED ANTIQUE ITALIAN CHANDELIER ILLUMINATES THE TABLE.

**ABOVE** A Louis XVI-
style walnut bergère
is paired with a William
IV-style library table.
Placed to elevate the
feet is the Louis XV
tabouret, circa 1760.

**OPPOSITE** Picking up
on the figures in the
toile de Jouy fabric
are lamps created
from English military
figures.

# A New Twist on Toile

PATTERNS APLENTY CREATE
A COZY OREGON ABODE.

**LEFT** PLANNED AS
CAREFULLY AS A PAINTING,
THE BREAKFAST NOOK
CHAIRS COMBINE LARGE
CHECKS WITH COLOR-
COORDINATED TOILE.

**OPPOSITE** CARRYING
OUT THE ROOM'S BLUE-
AND-WHITE THEME ARE
TRANSFERWARE PLATES
FROM THE HOMEOWNER'S
COLLECTION, WHICH ARE
USED FOR FAMILY MEALS
AS WELL AS TO DECORATE
WALLS.

**OPPOSITE** GROUNDED BY THE BARE FLOOR AND 19TH-CENTURY WOOD FURNITURE, THE MIX OF PATTERNS IN THE GARDEN-INSPIRED DINING ROOM HAS A HARMONIOUS RATHER THAN A JARRING EFFECT ON THE EYE.

**PAGES 102–103** AS BEAUTIFUL TO TOUCH AS TO SEE, TOILE, FLORAL, AND STRIPED FABRICS DOMINATE THE LIVING ROOM. THE DUTCH TEA TABLE COMPLEMENTS BOTH THE SCALE AND THE COLOR OF THE FURNITURE.

**i** "I love that French sense of style," says Gretchen Johnson, an artist and ardent Francophile. "I really like to feel a sense of order, but I also want it to be set up so you can just plop down and relax."

The best way to achieve this duet of desires in her new home in Lake Oswego, Oregon, was to decorate it *à la fran- çaise*. Passionate about fabric, especially the picturesque toiles of France, she decided to use them as the starting point, adding checks, florals, stripes, and animal prints. "I start with fabrics because I think when you find a fabric that you love, then it's easy to put all the other things together," she explains. (CONTINUED ON PAGE 104)

103

**LEFT** THE ANTIQUE BOOKCASE WAS GLAZED YELLOW TO BRING ATTENTION TO ITS LINING OF PROVINCIAL ANIMAL-PRINT FABRIC ALSO USED FOR THE SEATS OF THE ANTIQUE CHAIRS PLACED ON EACH SIDE.

**OPPOSITE** ONE OF GRETCHEN'S OWN PAINTINGS TOPS THE LIVING ROOM'S CONCRETE FIREPLACE MANTEL THAT WAS HAND-CARVED BY A LOCAL ARTISAN.

Choosing the colors to use was easy because of her special fondness for the rich blue seen so often on hand-thrown pottery in the south of France. A quick glance around the house proves that it works well: blue-and-white transferware displayed in the family room accentuates the blue-check chair and ottoman and deeply cushioned sofa covered in blue toile. In the breakfast nook, the chairs are covered in both toile and check, while the window valances exhibit a third blue-and-white pattern.

Gretchen also has a taste for mossy green. Combined with cream, it makes up the various patterns decorating the country-shuttered living room and more formal dining room. In the living room it is used strictly for the upholstery, whereas in the dining room, toile covers the walls and makes up the drapes. A fun leopard print on the chairs ringing the curvaceous 19th-century French walnut dining table balances the formality of the wallcovering with a contemporary note. A more classic floral blooms on two Louis-style accent chairs, and lights glow under gingham-checked shades.

(CONTINUED ON PAGE 109)

**RIGHT** THE SUNLIT BREAKFAST NOOK IS OUTFITTED WITH A 19TH-CENTURY FRENCH FRUITWOOD TABLE ORIGINALLY USED FOR WINE TASTINGS AND REPRODUCTION CHAIRS SIMILAR TO THOSE OF THE SAME PERIOD.

**OPPOSITE** DESIGNED FOR TIMELESS APPEAL AND FUNCTIONALITY, THE KITCHEN CENTERS ON A MARBLE-TOPPED ISLAND. PANELED CABINETS BELOW AND GLASS-FRONTED ONES ABOVE MAKE FOR EASY MEAL PREPARATION AND CLEANUP.

To highlight the fabrics and avoid aesthetic anarchy, Gretchen kept most of the polished hardwood floors bare. For the same reasons architectural accents, such as the fireplace, moldings, and interior shutters, were also kept subdued.

Always important to Gretchen's scheme is a room's functionality. The kitchen, for example, was renovated with glass-doored cabinetry to facilitate family cooking nights and quick cleanups. Its light-colored marble countertop appealed for both its beauty and usefulness. Although some might see marble's vulnerability to stains as a drawback, for Gretchen it adds to the charm. "You go to Paris and see these wonderful old marble counters that have been there forever," she says. "To me, that patina of use just adds to the character of a home."

**ABOVE** A RARE, FOUR-PANELED SCREEN, PINE TABLE, AND OUT-OF-THE-ORDINARY CARVED AND UPHOLSTERED CHAIR CREATE AN ELEGANT WRITING AREA IN THE MASTER SUITE.

**OPPOSITE** REPRODUCTION FRENCH TABLES ACT AS NIGHTSTANDS IN THE MASTER BEDROOM.

# Unabashedly Pretty

## A STATELY HOME LOOSENS UP WITH A PRETTY PALETTE OF PASTELS.

**LEFT** ADDING A FRESH NOTE THROUGHOUT THE HOUSE ARE HOME-GROWN ROSES. A SIMPLE MOUNDED BOUQUET SHOWS TO ADVANTAGE IN AN ANTIQUE CUT-GLASS VASE.

**OPPOSITE** A GILDED-AND-PAINTED ANTIQUE FRENCH CANAPÉ, OR SETTEE, IS UPDATED WITH A NEUTRAL FABRIC AND BRIGHT, SILK-COVERED PILLOWS.

**OPPOSITE** THE DOVE GRAY VESTIBULE LEADS TO THE GARDEN IN THE BACK OF THE HOUSE. ABOVE THE DOORWAY IS A GOLD-LEAFED AND PAINTED ARCHITECTURAL FRAGMENT. CUSTOM LEATHER BANDS THAT MATCH THE WALLS TRIM THE STAIR RUNNER.

**LEFT** A TALL GILT MIRROR, AN EIGHT-LEGGED SETTEE, AND FLOOR-TO-CEILING GRAY SILK PORTIERES CREATE AN AIR OF GRANDEUR.

**PAGE 114** GILT ACANTHUS-SHAPED FINIALS ADD GLAMOUR TO THE BUTTON-DETAILED, PLEATED DRAPERIES. THE DELICATE COLOR SCHEME USED THROUGHOUT CONTINUES WITH THE FRENCH BLUE AND GOLD-ACCENTED LAMP AND BUREAU.

**PAGE 115** RICHLY DECORATED WITH SUCH LIGHT-REFLECTING MATERIALS AS MARBLE, GOLD, AND SILK, THE LIVING ROOM ACHIEVES BALANCE BY PLAYING PATTERNS AGAINST SOLIDS.

As exquisite as the gowns worn at the fancy-dress balls depicted in Watteau's paintings, Laura and Ned Valentine's house in Richmond is an ode to romantic elegance. Fashioned with the same palette of colors—shell pink, alabaster, dove gray, and French blue—and similar fabrics—luscious silk, shimmering moiré, and rustling taffeta—their home is rich with antiques while retaining a feeling of genteel lightheartedness.

Designer Suellen Gregory began the makeover from the bottom up by stenciling oversize, gray and white diamonds on the floors. Simple yet striking, the geometric motif balances the abundance of curves on the painted furniture, voluptuously flowing draperies, and the undulant candelabra and sconces that dominate the furnishings. (CONTINUED ON PAGE 116)

In the dining room the walls are a pale, cool gray. Faux panels created with gold leaf and white paint add distinction. The effect is delicate and understated, the perfect backdrop for the strict lines of the table and oval-back, Louis XVI-style chairs. The floor-to-ceiling windows are dressed with shirred pink silk panels caught with an engraved metal tieback. And proving that ingenuity always wins out, Suellen explains how they came to be. "I looked and looked and finally went with a dress silk because I couldn't find the right color among drapery fabrics. I found it at a remnant store in Washington, D.C. ... a special order, possibly for a wedding, that someone had never picked up."

FLOORED IN THE SAME OVERSIZE STENCILED DIAMONDS AS THE FOYER, THE DINING ROOM FEATURES DELICATE FAUX PANELING WITH RECTANGLES OUTLINED IN GOLD LEAF AND WHITE PAINT.

**OPPOSITE** MATCHING THE DRAPERIES' NARROW STRIPES, THE GILT-FRAMED SCREEN PROPPED AGAINST THE WALL ADDS DIMENSION TO A CORNER OF THE FAMILY ROOM.

**RIGHT** DELIGHTING IN THEIR FRAGRANCE, LAURA PLACES BLOOMS FROM HER GARDEN THROUGHOUT THE HOUSE, HERE IN A SMALL SILVER BASKET.

Compensating for the residence's lack of structural details are large paintings with carved gilt frames, dramatic trumeau mirrors, and architectural salvage she had painted and gilded to add interest to the walls. And to prevent the decor from becoming too sweet, she and Laura, who prefers stripes over florals, chose different versions to use in several ways: an elegant, widely spaced, cream-and-gray for the antique French settee in the vestibule; bold and subdued in varying widths for pillows on the living room sofa; and a rose-and-cream pinstripe for the family room curtains.

In the bedrooms, pale pink and gray walls accented by white moldings and window frames bring in much-needed light. As elsewhere, accessories were crucial to create the look, with lavishly carved mirrors adding texture and dimension to the walls, antique French chandeliers creating sparkle, and lustrous bed linens discreetly seductive with dressmaker details.

Maintaining the delicate balance between just enough and too much demands a discerning eye and a careful hand. The Valentine home is a tribute to what a sensitive partnership between homeowner and designer can achieve.

**ABOVE** Gold-accented pink and flowers brighten Laura's daughter's room.

**OPPOSITE** The antique French chandelier and dressing table mirror introduce a hint of gilt to the tranquil master bedroom.

# Bold and Beautiful

WITH MOTHER NATURE AT HER SIDE, A FLORIDIAN DESIGNS A HOME AS BRIGHT AS THE GREAT OUTDOORS.

**LEFT** ARRANGED LIKE FRESH PRODUCE ON THE WINDOWSILL, THE LIMOGES PORCELAIN VEGETABLE BOXES PROVIDED PAM PANIELLO WITH INSPIRATION FOR HER KITCHEN'S COLOR SCHEME.

**OPPOSITE** VIBRANT SHADES ARE A HALLMARK OF PAM'S MANY PIECES OF ART-FAIR POTTERY USED FOR ENTERTAINING INSIDE AND OUT.

**OPPOSITE** BOLD PATTERNS SUIT THE OVERSIZE FURNITURE IN THE GENEROUSLY PROPORTIONED FAMILY ROOM. BEHIND THE SOFA, DISPLAYING COLORFUL CERAMICS, IS A LARGE FARM TABLE USED FOR DINNERS.

**RIGHT** BANQUETTES TURN A CORNER OF THE KITCHEN INTO A BREAKFAST NOOK.

Enter Pam Paniello's home in Tampa and you are instantly transported to a picnic in Provence. Bright with the sunny colors of freshly picked fruits and vegetables piled high in the outdoor food stalls throughout France, it is, in a word, "magic."

"I wanted it fun, colorful, and relaxing, not staid and stiff," she says of the house, which was built in the 1930s. "This is a pretty serious house, but I pushed it as far as I could." Awash with sunlight pouring in from the floor-to-ceiling arched windows and French doors, the large family room is a brilliant mix of banana-leaf green, pear yellow, cantaloupe orange, and a rich iris blue that converges beautifully with the fresh, apple green walls. Emboldening the colors' power and adding the final flourish to the room's composition is a jumble of patterns—huge bunches of fruit, brazen stripes, small-scale circles, and love knots.

**LEFT** PAINTED MARIGOLD YELLOW AND WASHED WITH GLAZE, THE REPRODUCTION WELSH CUPBOARD LOOKS LIKE AN OLD PIECE FROM PROVENCE.

**OPPOSITE** BEAUTIFULLY CRAFTED MILLWORK ENRICHES THE FRENCH BLUE CABINETRY AND IS REPEATED IN THE OVERHEAD BEAMS, WHICH ARE SET WITH PIN LIGHTS. THE MULTIDRAWER ISLAND MAKES FOOD PREPARATION A SNAP.

In the breakfast nook and kitchen, Pam followed the green scheme but took the intensity down several notches. In the nook, walls painted the same shade as a Granny Smith apple are tamed by demure checks and warm wood furniture. In the primarily French blue kitchen, green is an accent, used on small portions of the walls, the pleated window shade, and the art-fair pottery used for everyday meals.

**OPPOSITE** ECHOING THE AGED COLORS OF THE 18TH-CENTURY FRENCH ARMOIRE, THE CHINOISERIE FABRIC USED THROUGHOUT THE MASTER BEDROOM IS OFFSET BY BRICK RED AND WHITE BED LINENS. THE GILT-ACCENTED MIRROR ENLARGES THE ROOM WITH ITS REFLECTION.

**RIGHT** CUSHIONED WINDOW SEATS FLANKING THE FIREPLACE ARE PAINTED CREAM TO MATCH THE ROOM'S WOODWORK, BALANCING THE EXTRAVAGANT USE OF PATTERN.

As fearless with prints as she is with color, Pam immersed her master bedroom in a sea of flowers and figurative motifs. More mellow than the public rooms, this space is dominated by softened yellow, blue, and red. From curtains and walls to window seats and upholstered club chairs, nearly every inch, save the simple wood-manteled fireplace, is covered with a mustard, olive, and rose stripe that alternates chinoiserie designs with rows of cartouches, or framed motifs.

"People are afraid of making mistakes and choosing colors they'll tire of," she says with understanding. But there is a way to get around it. "Look up and down the hues. You can make any color work in some way. You may think you don't like pink, but fuchsia can be dynamite." Ever the pragmatist, Pam knows that even the most astute among us can blunder. In that case the solution is easy: Repaint.

# Touched
## by the Sun

## A DEFT MIX OF ELEGANT AND EASY BREATHES FRESH COUNTRY AIR INTO A SLICK CITY HOME.

**LEFT** COMPLEMENTING THE PEARWOOD ISLAND IS AN ANTIQUE CHILD'S WHEELBARROW, WHICH NOW HOLDS LINEN TEA TOWELS.

**OPPOSITE** THE LOG-CABIN PRINT ON THE CHAIR, A MODERN TAKE ON TRADITIONAL FRENCH TOILE DE JOUY, INSPIRED THE COLOR PALETTE OF THE ENTIRE HOUSE.

**ABOVE** THE ANTIQUE DOORS OPENING ONTO THE GREAT ROOM WERE FOUND IN A PARIS FLEA MARKET. MICKEY AGED THEM FURTHER WITH A PAINTED FINISH AND FRAMED THEM IN LIMESTONE SLABS.

**OPPOSITE** THE MIX OF COLORS, TEXTURES, AND PRINTS MAKES THE ROOM FEEL HOMEY YET ELEGANT.

It took 30 years of searching through French country fairs and flea markets, but today Mickey and Tom Harris's contemporary home in Tulsa is the idyllic Provençal-style cottage they had dreamed of.

"Country French will always be my first love," Mickey says. "It's sophisticated, yet it's casual." Plus, she adds, "Serious rooms are hard to live in." Emboldened by the insightful wisdom of interior designer Charles Faudree and surrounded by their collected treasures, she and Tom set out to create a home like the ones they had seen so often in France.

Aiming for "approachable elegance," they juxtaposed simple, painted wood pieces, such as an old oak commode, with highly polished ones carrying formidable pedigrees, such as the Louis XVI walnut armoire in the living room. In some instances, it was fabric that gave special pieces the rusticated look they coveted, as with the countrified checks and plaids used on an 1850 fruitwood sofa and a carved wing chair, both once clad in velvet. One especially fortuitous find was fabric patterned with Oklahoma log cabins that captured the colorful spirit of 18th-century French toile de Jouy. Used for the dining room chairs, it so delighted Mickey that she took its palette of warm golds, blues, and reds for the entire residence.

**ABOVE** Arranged above the Provençal-blue bureau are some of Mickey's collection of vintage French and English stitchery.

**OPPOSITE** A trumeau mirror and stone garden statue on the 17th-century limestone mantel lift the eye toward the high, timbered ceiling. The armoire is from the 1700s.

**ABOVE** FURNITURE
PLACEMENT DIVIDES THE
20×30-FOOT ROOM INTO
LIVING AND DINING AREAS.

**OPPOSITE**
STAFFORDSHIRE
FIGURINES AND
18TH-CENTURY PEWTER
LINE THE SHELVES OF
THE PROVENÇAL PLATE
RACK. IN FRONT AND
TO THE LEFT IS A
MARBLE-TOP PÂTISSERIE
TABLE USED AS A
SERVING PIECE.

Editing their collections to Mickey's "first loves," which include iconic French tôle chandeliers, creamware, and glistening trumeau mirrors, the couple assembled an artful mix for each room. Adding naïf English figurines of farm folks and cows and primitive toy wooden wheelbarrows, which Mickey keeps filled with flowers, assured her that all the senses would be satisfied.

For an up-country look, the walls in the public rooms were stuccoed and the ceilings vaulted with old beams and grape-stake fencing. Floors were stripped to the original concrete slab, then stained and scored to mimic stone, some laid with sisal area rugs, others left bare. Architectural elements such as arched windows and French doors were added for authenticity and interest.

**ABOVE** A SIMPLE FARM TABLE ANCHORS THE BREAKFAST BAY. THE 18TH-CENTURY CLOCK IS THOUGHT TO BE SWEDISH.

**OPPOSITE** UNDER THE PITCHED CEILING OF GRAPESTAKE FENCING, PROVINCIAL TREASURES INCLUDE A COW HEAD FROM A FRENCH BUTCHER'S SIGN AND A RAFFIA-COVERED WINE JUG.

Mickey used several old pieces in new ways or revamped them to better suit her needs: The vanity in the master bath was made from an antique bureau; the kitchen island had been a cashier's stand in a French shop. A fancifully carved plate rack, perhaps once decorating the wall of a French *maison*, was "married" to a dresser. As Mickey says, "It's the mix, not the match, so whatever you love, you can make it fit."

With the gems she and Tom have found, and more than a soupçon of talent, the Harris's home is homage to country living done right.

**ABOVE** TOPPED WITH MARBLE, THE 19TH-CENTURY BUREAU OF FAUX BAMBOO WAS TRANSFORMED INTO A VANITY FOR THE MASTER BATH.

**OPPOSITE** A MIX OF TOILES, STRIPES, AND PLAID GIVES THE MASTER BEDROOM A COZY FEEL. THE TÔLE CHANDELIER DATES FROM 1850.

**ABOVE** LAYERING PATTERN ON PATTERN, FRAMED STITCHERY AND BOTANICAL PRINTS ADORN THE GUEST ROOM WALL. THE UPHOLSTERED HEADBOARD ADDS A ROMANTIC TOUCH.

**OPPOSITE** MICKEY FOUND THE TALL FRENCH BONNETIÈRE, ORIGINALLY USED TO SHOWCASE HOSIERY, TO STORE TOWELS IN THE GUEST BATH.

# 3 Rustic Touches

# A Carefree Spirit

## A Southern accent puts a new spin on French decor.

LEFT Collected over the years, majolica is used throughout the house as a colorful accent.

OPPOSITE A porcelain Limoges box replicating the Eiffel Tower is a charming reminder of the city that inspired the home's decor.

**OPPOSITE** THE TRUMEAU MIRROR THAT BEGAN TRICIA'S LOVE AFFAIR WITH FRANCE HANGS ABOVE THE LIVING ROOM FIREPLACE.

**RIGHT** A TYPICALLY FRENCH MÉLANGE OF PATTERNS CREATES A COMFY MOOD. THE LAMPS WERE MADE FROM METAL STATUES.

"Even in the way they dress, the French have a flair for just throwing something together and not worrying about matching, and it always looks great," says Tricia Elve. "I've tried to follow that idea with my decorating."

Drawn to "the more casual look of French instead of the more formal English" since childhood, Tricia was living in Paris with husband Dave when, on her way to a farmer's market, she experienced a *coup de foudre,* as they say—and fell in love with a trumeau mirror in a small antiques shop. "I had to have it," she remembers, never imagining at the time that its purchase would lead her to open the French antiques consignment booth she now operates.

With the same "Southernized French" approach, as she calls it, that she uses for her booth, the Elves' house in Atlanta mixes 18th-century French pieces with primitive Southern ones. To set the stage, Dave refinished the floors and stained them a worn oak color to give them a centuries-old European look. Newly installed French doors and fireplaces and a coat of gray-green paint on the walls complete the setting. Tricia dressed the rooms with lots of cocoa-color cotton plaid interspersed with dashes of toile and buttery distressed leather on chairs and settees; the large-scale armoires, consoles, and desks brought home from France are positioned just so with the smaller Southern pieces.

The living room has carved pieces from both Georgia and France, along with some of the many paintings the couple picked up during their two-year stay in Paris. Favorite statues were transformed into lamps, and amusing mementos, such as a Limoges box in the shape of the Eiffel Tower, decorate surfaces. (CONTINUED ON PAGE 155)

ABOVE A COLLECTION OF COLORFUL, PRE-EURO FRENCH CURRENCY GATHERED IN ONE OF TRICIA'S MANY MAJOLICA BOWLS BRINGS TO MIND FOND MEMORIES OF PAST SOJOURNS IN FRANCE.

OPPOSITE FRINGED DAMASK DRAPES THE DINING TABLE. THE AUBUSSON RUG REFLECTS THE WARM TONES OF ANTIQUE WOOD FURNITURE AND SOFT YELLOW WALLS.

**ABOVE** Souvenirs such as the small Quimper bowl and photo of the Eiffel tower breathe French flair into every room.

**OPPOSITE** Purchased in Beaune, the capital of French wine country, the painting above the fireplace is just one of many in the room hung at various levels to add movement and capture the eye.

**ABOVE** PORCELAIN STAFFORDSHIRE POOCHES GUARD THE FAMILY FROM THE VANTAGE POINT OF AN 18TH-CENTURY FRENCH WALNUT CHEST.

**OPPOSITE** DECEPTIVELY SIMPLE WITH ITS MIX OF TEXTURES AND PATTERNS, THE GUEST BEDROOM REFLECTS TRICIA'S FONDNESS FOR MIXING CHECKS AND TOILE.

In the kitchen, Tricia put pine beams on the ceiling and chunky furniture in place of built-ins. From here, one walks to the more formal dining room that invites long dinners *à la française*. Carpeted with an Aubusson rug and dominated by a damask-draped table, the room features rustic notes such as a modestly carved antique French buffet, iron sconces replicating vine leaves, gingham draperies, and mustard-glazed earthenware from Provence.

As in a French country inn, the guest bedroom features one of Tricia's favorite decorating devices. "I have always loved the crisp, clean look of the check and how it works with French toile." To use the scheme, she padded the Regency-style headboard in a black, white, and yellow check and added boudoir pillows slipcovered in toile and edged with the same check. The dust ruffle repeats the pattern, picking up the check effect in the carpet.

Regal French and rustic country: With an experienced eye, the twain shall meet.

# Light & Shadow

The great outdoors plays a major role in the interior design of a Florida home.

**LEFT** Upholstered in bold stripes, the antique chair is a sophisticated partner for the dining table layered with a frothy confection.

**OPPOSITE** Vintage paintings in their original frames add textural excitement to a hallway tableau.

Built in 1922, in the very middle of the Art Nouveau period, Elizabeth Gibson-Wakeman's home in Sarasota, Florida, features a sublime blend of the curvilinear designs of that era with the white-painted wicker that one would expect in a contemporary home in the tropics.

A transplant from the Northeast, Elizabeth, who has been in the design field for more than two decades, says, "Moving to Sarasota liberated me as a designer. I spend a lot of time judging light and shadows. It's important to create seating areas where you're going to be comfortable at the time of day you want to use them." Applying the same principle to her own remodel as she would to a client's, she created a breakfast spot that basks in morning light and a cocktail area that looks out to views of the pool sparkling in the fading twilight. She also enclosed a porch to make a library for her husband, who uses it around the clock.

LEFT THE RECTANGULAR SCREEN PORCH WAS DIVIDED INTO A LIBRARY AND A SITTING ROOM. CARVED CEILING PLAQUES, SALVAGED FROM A FRENCH CHÂTEAU, HANG ABOVE THE TURN-OF-THE-CENTURY SETTEE.

OPPOSITE FROM THE FIVE SHADES OF WHITE ON THE WALLS AND TOBACCO-STAINED HARDWOOD FLOOR TO THE ORNATE CHANDELIER ABOVE AND SLEEK STRIPES ON THE CHAIRS, THE DINING ROOM IS A STUDY IN CONTRASTS.

Also integral to her design theory is correctly sizing each space for its intended use. To this end she reduced the original, grandly scaled dining room to better suit her nearly daily gatherings of six and enlarged the kitchen to comfortably seat eight, which is the number she invites for more formal dinners.

The living room expresses another dictum: "To enhance something, you have to surround it with open space." Painted in many shades of white—molding gets two or three closely aligned variants, walls and ceiling are slightly darker, doors still another, with each tint determined by how the light from outdoors affects the surface at different times of the day and night—it features a cluster of club and slipper chairs along with a big pouf upholstered in off-white damask and three very fine 19th-century French pieces. Against the palette of whites and sisal rug underfoot, the spare lines and floral inlay of the chest and graceful turn of the tulip-shaped cocktail table take on sculptural importance.

Touches of subtle elegance associated with the grand homes of Paris are sprinkled throughout, some in rather offbeat places. The kitchen, for one, which is as hardworking as they

**OPPOSITE**
PRACTICALITY GUIDED
THE SELECTION OF GRAY
FOR THE CABINETS
RATHER THAN WHITE,
BUT GLAMOUR WON OUT
WITH DRAPERIES MADE
TO MATCH THOSE IN THE
EATING AREA OF THE
KITCHEN-DINING ROOM.

**RIGHT** A LARGE ISLAND
SEPARATES THE WORKING
SIDE OF THE KITCHEN
FROM THE DINING SIDE.
FACING THE TABLE ARE
A WARMING OVEN AND
DRAWERS.

come, is dressed up with gracefully puddling drapes. "I spend a lot of time in my kitchen," Elizabeth explains, "and I want it to feel as good to me as all the other rooms." In the small sunroom, furnished in 1890s wicker and rustic painted-wood pieces, two trapezoidal carved ceiling plaques salvaged from a French château contrast with the vertically paneled walls.

Accessorized by faux bamboo furniture from the turn of the century, vintage paintings, and her towering phalaenopsis orchids, it's easy to see why an invitation chez Elizabeth is coveted among friends and family alike.

# Inspired Simplicity

## Combining old with new brings life to a tiny country cottage.

**LEFT** Unbleached canvas upholstery focuses attention on the romantic patina of an antique chair.

**OPPOSITE** Everyday items in the kitchen are displayed as precisely as fine art.

**OPPOSITE** Extra living space was created by enclosing the front porch. The stone walls and floor provide the perfect backdrop for Caroline and Jon-Paul's mix of rustic and formal pieces.

**PAGES 168–169** Glamorized by the antique pier mirror, the living room works hard too. The wicker trunk hides toys, slipcovers are washable, and it's easy to sweep the bleached wood floor.

1

Like an atelier under the eaves of a Parisian rooftop, the home of Caroline Verschoor and Jon-Paul Saunier includes old and new, handmade and store-bought. Owners of a shop that sells European finds for the home and garden, they've turned their stone cottage in northern Virginia into a lesson in creativity.

"I cannot emphasize enough that each house has its own unique demands," says Caroline, and theirs was no exception. "A little dumpy," as she recalls, but set on a beautiful swath of land, it was half the size of the contemporary loft she and Jon had left behind in metropolitan Washington, D.C. Marked by small windows and dark interiors, it was not the setting for the colorful decor Caroline would have liked. Instead, knowing that adaptation is often the wiser choice, she painted most of the interior white: The ceiling, which is less than eight feet, would then appear higher, and the dingy rooms, not large to begin with, would look brighter. She also sanded and bleached the wood floors, which were left bare in much of the house. (CONTINUED ON PAGE 170)

**LEFT** BLACK-AND-WHITE TRANSFERWARE FORMS A STILL LIFE WITH AN OLD CHICKEN FEEDER THAT HAS BEEN FILLED WITH SAND AND VOTIVE CANDLES.

**OPPOSITE** THE SLIGHTLY DISTRESSED KITCHEN CABINETRY HARMONIZES WITH THE ORIGINAL CEILING BEAMS AND TILED FLOOR. AN OLD PAINTING FRAMED IN GOLD ADDS AN UNEXPECTED FOCAL POINT.

Mirrors hang in myriad ways to capture and reflect the sunlight: A small one framed by a gold sunburst is propped on a bookshelf, medium-size convex beauties hang on walls, and an enormous antique pier mirror is used as it would have been in the 1700s, placed between two windows and paired with a table. Modish, low-voltage lights snake along the ceiling among the white-painted beams, cabinets are kept open, and much of the furniture, both rustic farm and dressy French, is covered with a creamy, unbleached linen or a toile Caroline had soaked in tea to achieve a soft, ecru shade. Most important to the design of the house are the paintings and sculpture that Caroline and Jon had collected over the years. "I think art, when it speaks to you, is priceless," says Caroline. (CONTINUED ON PAGE 174)

BUILT-IN SHELVES
WERE ADDED TO HOLD
EVERYTHING FROM
UNUSED CHINA TO BOOKS
AND FILES. ROMAN
SHADES FINISH THE
LOOK WHILE ALLOWING IN
MAXIMUM LIGHT.

**LEFT** ONE OF THE PLEASURES OF DEALING IN ANTIQUES IS THE PRIVILEGE OF LIVING WITH THE OBJECTS BEFORE PASSING THEM ALONG TO NEW OWNERS.

**OPPOSITE** A SALVAGED, PEELING COLUMN ADDS TEXTURE TO THE DINING ROOM AS DO THE RAFFIA CHAIRS. PUNCTUATED WITH FOGGY GRAY, THE LOOK IS STRAIGHT FROM FRANCE'S BRITTANY COAST.

Bringing the outside in is characteristic of homes in the French countryside, where the distinction between the two often blurs. Caroline and Jon achieved that blending with exposed stone walls, unadorned windows, and that turn-of-the-century favorite, ferns, positioned on lacy wire stands. And with the addition of wicker and faux bamboo pieces underscored by nubby sisal rugs, Caroline added an authentically natural touch and just enough texture to make it interesting. The result is a divine little home filled with objects to love, cherish, and enjoy daily.

**ABOVE** THE OLD-FASHIONED BATHTUB FEATURES A EUROPEAN "TELEPHONE SHOWER" THAT HOOKS OVER THE FAUCET WHEN NOT IN USE.

**OPPOSITE** LOOKING TYPICALLY TURN-OF-THE-CENTURY FRENCH, THE BEDROOM BOASTS A CONTEMPORARY LEATHER CHAIR CAMOUFLAGED BY TOILE AND A ROMANTIC CANOPY OVER THE BED IMPORTED FROM THE NETHERLANDS.

# Naturally Magnifique

## A BIT OF FRANCE COMES TO LIFE IN THE HISTORIC HEART OF AMERICA.

LEFT FOUND IN A FLEA MARKET, THE PAINTED WOOD ROOSTER SURVEYS THE BREAKFAST NOOK.

OPPOSITE THE MASSIVE FIREPLACE LOOKS OLD BUT IS NEW TO THE RADICALLY REMODELED HOUSE. A LARGE POSTER ADVERTISING A FRENCH BUTTER COOKIE HANGS AS ART BETWEEN THE WINDOWS.

**OPPOSITE** THE MASSIVE VERMONT FIELDSTONE FIREPLACE IS THE HEART OF THE GREAT ROOM. THE PICKLED OAK TABLE IS 19TH-CENTURY FRENCH. CUSHIONED RUSH CHAIRS ARE FROM MARY'S SHOP.

**ABOVE** BUILT IN THE 1920S, THE RESIDENCE FORMERLY SERVED AS CARRIAGE HOUSE, STABLE, CARETAKERS' QUARTERS, AND GREENHOUSE.

b

Built in the 1920s, Mary and George Harrington's carriage house, stable, caretakers' quarters, and greenhouse required a total redo before it could be called "home."

Located north of Boston, where Mary runs Lavender Home and Table, a favorite design shop on fashionable Newbury Street, the house hadn't been lived in for a year. "It was a mess," she says. The floors in the main room had been covered with linoleum, the wooden ceiling beams painted white, and the walls masked with plywood. Add to that a strange layout—three small rooms made up the kitchen, while there was only one small bedroom on the second floor—and it was obvious that a dramatic change and lots of hard work would be required, especially if they were to create a home with subtle French flair.

To accommodate their family of four and provide room for entertaining, Mary and George decided to create one expansive space on the ground floor. It would incorporate living and dining rooms as well as a large kitchen that would invite family participation in food preparation. And it would encourage guests to pull up a chair and enjoy a glass of wine.

"We felt the room needed something with mass to it, so we added the fireplace," explains Mary. The oak mantel on the fieldstone front was stained a rich brown to match the custom mahogany French doors and arched transoms that fill the original carriage door openings along one wall. The painted wood beams were restored, and antique limestone, salvaged from several French farmhouses, was laid for the floor.

Serving as a backdrop for some marvelous French collectibles, including an Art Nouveau *affiche*, or poster, advertising a favorite cookie, the walls were plastered, then painted three times to achieve an aged look. Casual in the way it has been arranged, the 19th-century antique furniture in the living area includes a well-worn leather sofa and two matching wing chairs and a solid-wood coffee table found in a French flea market. A French vintner's table serves as a bar, and the rustic shelving placed upon it displays the couple's collection of antique duck decoys.

For meals there's a 19th-century French pickled oak table and comfortably cushioned rush-seated chairs from Mary's shop. Hanging above both living and dining areas is a pair of antique copper French streetlights, while 1920s-era French lights adorn the wall.

A brick courtyard in front of the house and a bluestone terrace in back complete the transfiguration. Hinting of the rustic pleasures of Provence, the house and its furnishings will continue to acquire a patinated gleam, fine-tuned every day by this happy family.

# With an
# Artist's Eye

ON THE HIGH PLAINS AN ARTIST TURNS HER DREAM INTO REALITY.

**LEFT** A TRIO OF VASES BY DENVER ARTIST MARIO RIVOLI STANDS ON AN 1880S FRENCH BURLED TABLE IN THE ENTRY HALL.

**OPPOSITE** BLUE AS THE PROVENÇAL SKY, THE GUEST ROOM'S FRENCH BED IS DRESSED WITH A FAMILY QUILT AND PILLOWS COVERED IN ANTIQUE TICKING. AN OLD HOOKED RUG ADDS WARMTH TO THE WIDE-PLANKED FLOOR.

**OPPOSITE** SETTING THE FRENCH TONE OF THE HOUSE IN THE ENTRY HALL ARE AN OLD FRENCH MOVIE POSTER, AN 1880S BURLED-WOOD SIDE TABLE, AND A SALVAGED COLUMN.

**BELOW** WITH ITS GALVANIZED METAL ROOF, BARN-LIKE SHUTTERS, AND STUCCO EXTERIOR, "LA BASTIDE" RESEMBLES A PROVENÇAL FARMHOUSE.

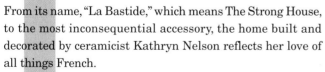

From its name, "La Bastide," which means The Strong House, to the most inconsequential accessory, the home built and decorated by ceramicist Kathryn Nelson reflects her love of all things French.

Situated in a Colorado wheat field surrounded by woods and nestled near a stream, this rustic country farmhouse Kathryn shares with Steve Scobee captures her view on how the French mix and match so well. "The French are very ethnic-oriented and comfortable putting things from all over the world together, and they aren't afraid to blend old and new," she says. "Everything looks so effortless, and that's what I wanted to do here."

Starting with the stucco exterior, Kathryn wanted her house to look as though "cows had rubbed their backs on (the walls) for years." The galvanized metal roof and barnwood shutters add to the centuries-old feel and remind one of farmhouses in the Midi region of France, which are handed down from generation to generation. Inside, her artistic sense went into overdrive as she selected the tints for the color-infused plaster wall treatments. "The colors of Provence are so beautiful. How could you not have a yellow and a blue and a green and a white?" A creamy ecru suggesting old muslin was used for the living room, entry, kitchen, and hallways. A deep clear blue and a warm gold, like that decorating the pottery of Quimper, were used for two guest rooms, and the master bedroom glows with an ocher that subtly changes with the light.

**ABOVE** ENLIVENED BY A KILIM RUG, THE LIVING ROOM'S NEUTRAL PALETTE SHOWS OFF ARTWORK TO ADVANTAGE.

**OPPOSITE** THE GRAND FIREPLACE, FRAMED BY A FOUND MANTEL, CASTS A GLOW ON THE CUSTOM-FORGED IRON TABLES. NATURAL LINEN COVERS THE SOFAS, AND THE ANTIQUE WALNUT CHAIRS WEAR WHITE MUSLIN.

OPPOSITE BATHED
IN SUNSHINE, THE
BREAKFAST ROOM
IS PACKED WITH AN
ECLECTIC SELECTION OF
DECORATIVE WARES FROM
FOREIGN COUNTRIES. THE
CHAIRS ARE FROM
19TH-CENTURY
FRANCE, THE BLUE 1780
CUPBOARD IS FROM
CANADA, AND THE DARK
GREEN SHELF ON THE
LEFT WAS MADE IN 1889 IN
MEXICO.

LEFT "I WANTED
EVERYTHING TO LOOK
LIKE FURNITURE,"
SAYS KATHRYN OF THE
KITCHEN. TILES FORM THE
STOVE'S BACKSPLASH,
AND UNPOLISHED
BLACK SLATE TOPS THE
CABINETRY.

Beams foraged from old barns were installed and concrete floors poured to tie the main-level spaces together. As construction progressed, the search for old cupboards, architectural salvage, fireplace mantels, and antique doors began in earnest. Not one to be put off by challenges, Kathryn told her architect, "form follows furniture." Thus it was the house plan that had to change when she unhappily realized that the antiques she was acquiring required two extra feet in the living room and wider hallways.

Centered around the kitchen, the Y-shape floor plan includes a cozy library but no dining room. "I never used the dining room in my last house, so I decided not to include one here," Kathryn explains. Instead, guests gather around the breakfast table in the kitchen or in the library, where blue- and green-washed woodwork and shelves laden with books and collectibles create a delightful setting for relaxing dinner parties that last late into the night.

(CONTINUED ON PAGE 195)

**ABOVE** AN UNPAINTED BENCH FROM INDONESIA PROVIDES A RESTING SPOT IN THE LOGGIA. METAL LANTERNS OFFER TEXTURAL CONTRAST TO THE WOOD FURNITURE AND ADD A COZY GLOW WHEN LIGHTED.

**OPPOSITE** USED OFTEN FOR SMALL DINNER PARTIES, THE LIBRARY IS PAINTED VARIATIONS OF THE SUN-KISSED BLUES AND GREENS FOUND ON THE CÔTE D'AZUR.

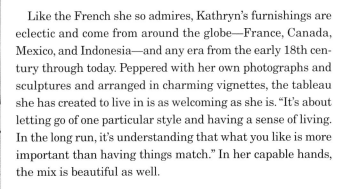

Like the French she so admires, Kathryn's furnishings are eclectic and come from around the globe—France, Canada, Mexico, and Indonesia—and any era from the early 18th century through today. Peppered with her own photographs and sculptures and arranged in charming vignettes, the tableau she has created to live in is as welcoming as she is. "It's about letting go of one particular style and having a sense of living. In the long run, it's understanding that what you like is more important than having things match." In her capable hands, the mix is beautiful as well.

**OPPOSITE** AN ANTIQUE FRENCH CHILD'S BED SERVES AS A SETTEE AT THE FOOT OF THE CUSTOM IRON BED. FRAMED PRINTS FROM PARIS HANG ABOVE THE HEADBOARD.

**PAGE 196** A VICTORIAN-ERA DÉCOUPAGE SCREEN ENHANCES THE OLD-FASHIONED FEEL OF A GUEST ROOM.

**PAGE 197** AN IRON BED FROM A FRENCH CONVENT, PAINTED TO RESEMBLE WOOD, IS COVERED WITH A BOUTIS, A TYPE OF REVERSIBLE QUILT PARTICULAR TO PROVENCE, AND A DUVET MADE OF ANTIQUE FABRIC. THE PEWTER LAMP ON THE SMALL TABLE IS ALSO FRENCH.

# 4 Comfortably Chic

# Joie deVivre

Filled with natural light and antiques collected over 30 years, a California home embodies the art of living well à la française.

LEFT A garden sculpture from the 1920s adds a graceful touch to a salvaged column displayed in the dining room.

OPPOSITE Regal mixes with rustic. The large table was once used by a French butcher for curing meat—its lid lifts off to expose a trough. Flanking it are two 18th-century, triangular-shape half tables. The French field basket beneath holds architectural fragments.

Interior designer Lucinda Lester has been in love with all things French since she was a little girl. "My mother was passionate about French style, and it was catching," she explains. Thanks to that passion, combined with her own gift for creating beautiful living spaces, the Montecito, California, home she shares with husband Walter Owen could easily be mistaken for one situated in the French countryside.

Like a typical French house, it exudes a village-like warmth without giving up any city sophistication. Furnished with comfy, down-filled chairs and sofa and tables judiciously placed for a book or cup of tea, the home also has an air of old-world glamour with exquisite gilt mirrors and framed artwork.

"It's very French just to enjoy life," says Lucinda, "which means homes are not too perfect." Evidence of this is how the house was created, "... not put together in a six-month period, it's been collected over many years." For her eclectic mix of furnishings Lucinda chose a neutral backdrop: softly painted walls, simple floor-length curtains, and terra-cotta floor tiles set in a characteristically French herringbone pattern. White-painted wood and sisal rugs are used to define spaces. (CONTINUED ON PAGE 206)

OPPOSITE LUCINDA CREATED A BEAUTIFUL AND UNUSUALLY FUNCTIONAL FRONT DOOR BY FITTING 10-FOOT-TALL ANTIQUE IRON GATES WITH GLASS PANELS, WHICH CAN BE OPENED AND CLOSED. EIGHTEENTH-CENTURY FRENCH SHUTTERS STAND BEHIND THE SOFA. A TÔLE TRAY PROTECTS AND ADDS INTEREST TO THE COFFEE TABLE.

ABOVE LEFT SURROUNDED WITH PLANTS AND EDGED IN OLD ROCKS, THE POOL TAKES ON THE LOOK OF A FREE-FORM POND.

ABOVE ONCE AT HOME IN A FRENCH GARDEN, THE CONCRETE CUPID TABLE HOLDS AN OLIVE JAR GLAZED IN THE TRADITIONAL MUSTARD TONES OF PROVENCE.

PAGES 204–205 THE SLIPPER CHAIRS, DRESSED UP WITH SKIRTS AND TUFTED BACKS, AND THE CURVY COFFEE TABLE BRING A SOFT EDGE TO THE ROOM. TERRA-COTTA TILES LAID IN A TYPICAL FRENCH HERRINGBONE PATTERN ADD A RUSTIC TOUCH.

**LEFT** Among the many references to the out-of-doors are the gilt-framed painting by William Dorsey, the iron patio table on which it rests, and the viburnum-filled concrete urn.

**OPPOSITE** Flanked by gilt sconces, the 18th-century gold-leaf mirror lends a formal tone to the room where Lucinda and Walter like to relax at the end of the day. The chair on the right is also from the 1700s.

Among the 18th-century tables and chairs found on shopping trips to France, Lucinda mixed in garden sculptures, weathered shutters, and old urns. Inserting a casual note, these simple items also balance out the formal pieces. The result is that nothing is too precious, and everything can be enjoyed every day.

Much of the furniture is oversize, for as Lucinda remarks, "One large piece reads better than a lot of little ones sometimes." Some of them pull double duty as well, like the French ottoman in her bedroom measuring four feet long. Topped with a cushion, it's seating; without it, she has a coffee table. (CONTINUED ON PAGE 210)

**OPPOSITE** INSPIRED BY ARTWORK SEEN IN PARIS, THE TOPIARIES ARE PAINTED ON BURLAP STRETCHED OVER WOOD PANELS. RINGING THE TABLE ARE CHAIRS FROM 19TH-CENTURY FRANCE, FITTED WITH SILK-COVERED CUSHIONS.

**LEFT** RUSTIC SHUTTERS STAND AGAINST THE DINING ROOM WALL, ADDING AN INTERESTING DIMENSION. AGAINST THIS BACKDROP, A 1920S GARDEN SCULPTURE ON A SALVAGED PORCH COLUMN AND REPRODUCTION FRENCH CHAIR CREATE AN ELEGANT STILL LIFE.

Another trick used throughout the house appealing to both eye and hand is the cosmopolitan mix of textures. Exemplifying this perfectly is the dining room, its table layered with a scalloped-edged square over a crisp linen cloth and rough, caned-back 19th-century chairs from France cushioned in silk. To the side, a freestanding naïve artwork presents painted burlap over wood, which adds even more contrast to the mélange. Each detail taken alone would be interesting. Used together they create a tableau of striking beauty.

"I think our homes are so important to us," Lucinda says. "Even if we're not there, we know that place is our center, and we hold it in our mind's eye." It's obvious from this house that no matter where Lucinda is in the world, it is treasured in her eye and in her heart.

**OPPOSITE** A FANCIFUL GARDEN BENCH AND A PAIR OF 18TH-CENTURY FRENCH CHAIRS UPHOLSTERED IN THEIR ORIGINAL FABRIC CREATE A CONVERSATION CORNER IN THE BEDROOM. A SISAL RUG LAYERS TEXTURE OVER THE PAINTED FLOOR.

**PAGE 212–213** THE BED FROM 1800S FRANCE FEATURES CARVED BOWS AND FLOWERS AND A CANED AND PADDED FOOTBOARD.

**TOP** AN ANTIQUE LIMOGES PITCHER IS KEPT FILLED WITH FRESH FLOWERS.

**OPPOSITE** PURCHASED IN FRANCE, THE BEDROOM'S ARMOIRE HIDES A TV BEHIND ITS TOILE-COVERED PANELS. ANTIQUE FRENCH CHAIRS WITH GOLD-ACCENTED SUEDE SEATS DRAW UP TO THE CANE-TOPPED TABLE.

# Farm
# Fresh

A CHICAGO COUPLE FINDS PEACE STYLING THEIR HOMESTEAD WITH THE DELIGHTS OF RURAL FRANCE.

**LEFT** WITH WINDOWS ON ALL FOUR SIDES, THE BELVEDERE ATOP THE ROOF COMMANDS AN EXTRAORDINARY VIEW OF THE COUNTRYSIDE.

**OPPOSITE** THE HALLWAY IN THE GUEST WING IS DECORATED WITH ANTIQUE FARM PARAPHERNALIA, INCLUDING A HORSE-HEAD SIGN PROBABLY ONCE USED TO ADVERTISE A HARNESSMAKER'S SHOP

"It's a folly I carried around in my head," says Suzy Stout, explaining the French stone farmhouse situated next to a pond that she and husband Sam dreamed of having one day. Inspired by the desire to step back from a world that was "too much with us," the dwelling they built near Chicago reflects Suzy's vision of a home that included "the romance, softness, and spirituality of the past ... a truly enlightened farmhouse."

Designed with the help of architect Michael Graham, the "big 'small' house," as she calls it, is a little French, a little Midwestern, and a lot of fun—it's actually a cluster of barn-like structures that look more like a farm complex than a single residence. Painted white, set against green meadows and blue sky, the house, guest and master bedroom wings, and garage are postcard perfect, as are the interiors designed with French antiques, pieces acquired from hither and yon, and the colors and patterns found in Provence.

(CONTINUED ON PAGE 222)

**OPPOSITE** "WE WANTED THE POND BECAUSE WE LOVE LISTENING TO THE FROGS AND ALL THE POND NOISES," SAYS SUZY. IT'S STOCKED WITH FISH FOR EXTRA ENJOYMENT.

**ABOVE** THE CLUSTER OF BUILDINGS INCLUDES THE 3,500-SQUARE-FOOT HOUSE WITH TWO WINGS, AND AT LEFT, A GARAGE WHOSE ARCHED ENTRY LEADS INTO THE INNER COURTYARD.

**PAGE 220** BRINGING ATTENTION TO THE BELVEDERE AND HIGH-PEAKED CEILING IN THE ENTRANCE HALL ARE AN ANTIQUE LIGHT FIXTURE AND RUSTY STEEL CHANDELIER.

**PAGE 221** A PAIR OF ANTIQUE COLUMNS SEPARATES THE ENTRY HALL FROM THE LIVING ROOM. SUZY BOUGHT THE BENCH OFF THE BACK OF A TRUCK AT A FLEA MARKET.

Relaxed and gracious, the living room embodies the spirit Suzy set out to instill. Floored in mellow old pine, the room is wrapped in soft, mossy green walls that lead up to a pitched ceiling. Large windows and French doors are left uncovered. "I wanted every bit of the view to be a part of this room," she says. There are lots of flowering plants, and the furniture is upholstered in a mix of sage chenille and toile patterned with an old-fashioned pastoral scene. "It's a very undecorated room," she adds. "I think people often mistakenly think that it is great decorating if they get a fabulous fabric, a wonderful drapery design, or an incredible rug. Certainly those things are important, but more important are proportions and accessories."

(CONTINUED ON PAGE 226)

**ABOVE** THE LIVING ROOM'S CAREFULLY DESIGNED UNDECORATED LOOK IS EMPHASIZED BY THE SHINY BARE FLOOR AND ANTIQUE WOOD FIREPLACE MANTEL.

**OPPOSITE** ADDING A QUIRKY, AND VERY SOPHISTICATED, SHOT OF ELEGANCE TO THE COUNTRY-FRESH ROOM IS THE SPARKLING CRYSTAL CHANDELIER.

**OPPOSITE** THE KITCHEN'S WORK AREA EXHIBITS EXQUISITE ATTENTION TO DETAIL: BLUE CUPBOARD INTERIORS COMPLEMENT THE TILES; DRAWER PULLS MIX SHAPES AS WELL AS MATERIALS; THE STOVE HOOD GRACEFULLY DRAWS IT ALL TOGETHER.

**RIGHT** OPPOSITE THE KITCHEN'S WORK AREA, FAMILY AND FRIENDS LOVE TO GATHER AROUND THE FIRE. CHECKED LINEN DRAPERIES AND OVERSIZE FLORALS ON THE FURNITURE COZY UP THE LARGE ROOM.

This French point of view works as well everywhere else in the house. In the kitchen/family room—there is no formal dining room—nestled into a windowed bay is an antique French wine-tasting table ringed by six chairs found at a resale shop. Adjacent is a snug sitting area clustered around the huge fireplace. Pulling the two areas together are the antique French hexagonal terra-cotta tiled floor, mustard yellow walls, and blue-check draperies.

For holiday gatherings and serious entertaining, Suzy uses the 16×28-foot entry hall. Furnished with family heirlooms, including an antique needlework-covered chair and a French buffet, it has an aged feeling thanks to faux-finished walls. Two weathered columns were installed just inside the door-way for a note of enduring permanence.

"I think every house should be full of things you love," notes Suzy, "things that make you smile." This house clearly is.

**OPPOSITE** CONTINUING THE BLUE-AND-WHITE THEME IN THE KITCHEN/ DINING AREA ARE THE CUSHIONED CHAIRS. FOUND IN A RESALE SHOP, THEY SURROUND AN ANTIQUE FRENCH WINE-TASTING TABLE.

**PAGE 228** THE MASTER BEDROOM IS FURNISHED WITH FAMILY HEIRLOOMS AND FLEA-MARKET FINDS.

**PAGE 229** INSPIRED BY THE BATHS OF THE HOTEL RITZ IN THE 1930S, SUZY'S BATH PULLS OFF A PURE AND MODERN LOOK TOUCHED WITH OLD-FASHIONED FEMININITY.

# Romance Redux

## Love blossoms in a couple's country retreat.

LEFT ANTIQUE SCONCES AND A TRUMEAU MIRROR FOUND IN NEW ORLEANS GRACE ONE OF THE LIVING ROOM'S TWO FIREPLACES.

OPPOSITE THE BIANCHIS ENJOY INTIMATE TÊTE-À-TÊTES IN FRONT OF THE FIREPLACE IN THEIR BEDROOM. THE PRINTS AND FIREPLACE SCREEN ARE BY PARIS-TRAINED ARTIST MARCEL VERTES.

f

From the trumeau mirrors and a zinc bathtub from 1860s France to the chicken coop filled with Mille Fleur bantams and guarded by Centime the cat, the house that Penny and Adam Bianchi built in Montecito, California, is French country inside and out.

Set on a parcel of land just 65 feet square and surrounded by woods, the main house was constructed from the ground up, along with a guest cottage and separate garage, all clustered around a courtyard and garden. With "about 60 rolls of film of crooked roofs and lime-washed walls" that the couple had taken in the south of France, architect David Serrurier set to work.

**OPPOSITE** CLEVERLY BUILT INTO THE BAY WINDOW TO SAVE SPACE, THE SOFA IS FRAMED WITH AN ANTIQUE VALANCE AND VOILE CURTAINS.

# ROMANCE REDUX

The exteriors were fashioned of plaster mixed with pale sienna pigment, while the roof tiles, made by hand and shaped one by one over the craftsman's thigh, were placed in the same angular way they are in France. They were left unglazed to allow moss to grow—another detail that adds to the overall pastoral look. Because she couldn't find antique shutters, Penny employed a carpenter to make new ones. Guided by photos of Penny's favorites in Provence, he also sandblasted them and left them out in the rain for a while to acquire a weathered verdigris finish.

Being empty nesters, Penny says, "We wanted a couple's house." Her goal was to "keep love alive by creating a home filled with warmth and beauty, good food, and wine." And of course, graceful furniture and family heirlooms, the couple's extensive art collection, and lots of antique cottons. "I love these beautiful prints, the handmade look and the fineness of the detailing." So much so that Penny alternates them periodically. "Almost every seating piece in the house is slip-covered, and I change the covers at the beginning of October. The change of slipcovers, throws, and bedspreads is a wonderful, old-fashioned way of getting your home ready for the change of seasons."

**OPPOSITE** A GARDEN OF FLORALS TEMPERED WITH STRIPES AND ACCENTED BY ANIMAL PRINTS AND POLKA DOTS, THE LIVING ROOM IS ALIVE WITH COLOR. PENNY'S BOLD PALETTE IS THE PERFECT COMPLEMENT TO HER ART COLLECTION.

While much of the predominantly European furniture has formal lines, it takes on a rustic note dressed in an array of flowers, stripes, checks, and even needlepoint. A color scheme of sunny yellows and reds, hushed by blues that range from deep cadet to pastel cerulean, imbues the rooms with inviting warmth.

Covered with vines and complemented by lacy white iron benches, the house is as Penny wanted it to be: "comforting … (not) too decorated or too contrived." Certainly it is a place for love to grow and flourish.

**ABOVE** AT THE FAR END OF THE DRIVE IS THE GUEST COTTAGE. TO THE LEFT IS THE MAIN HOUSE AND TO THE RIGHT THE GARAGE. THE TILE-ROOFED, PLASTER EXTERIOR IS TYPICAL OF HOUSES IN PROVENCE.

**OPPOSITE** WITH ACCESS TO THE GARDEN THROUGH FRENCH DOORS, THE KITCHEN EMPHASIZES THE COUNTRY LOOK WITH ITS ROUGH TERRA-COTTA FLOOR, VINTAGE COTTON-SKIRTED ISLAND, AND GLEAMING COPPER POTS.

# A European Sensibility

## Cupids, curves, and character add romance to a Sonoma cottage.

**LEFT** Adding glamour to the master bedroom's dressing table is a sterling silver mirror draped with glass beads from the 1920s.

**OPPOSITE** The gentle lines of the French table and velvet-cushioned Italian chairs set a serene mood for the dining room.

**LEFT** AGLOW WITH THE FIRE'S FLAMES AND RICHLY ORNAMENTED ACCESSORIES, THE LIVING ROOM COMBINES ROMANCE WITH TRANQUILLITY. THE CIRCA-1906 MIRROR CONTRASTS WITH THE STRICT LINES OF THE CONCRETE AND VERMICULITE MANTEL.

Situated in a historic section of enchanting Sonoma, California, the century-old house appealed to Lorraine and Ben Egidios on many levels—but not for its dark 1970s-style interior. Lorraine, a designer and antiques dealer, and Ben, who has a talent for architecture, knew that transforming the cottage would be neither fast nor easy.

First on the to-do list was divesting the living room of its wood paneling, wood-burning stove, and balcony. Then, based on Ben's plan, contractors added a breakfast room, master suite, guest room, and powder room. With the structure revitalized and a good flow from room to room assured, the couple put their energy into decorating.

**OPPOSITE** AN ARCHITECTURAL FRAGMENT CROWNING THE ANTIQUE SECRÉTAIRE IN THE DINING ROOM REFLECTS THE DECORATION AT THE TOP OF THE LOUIS XVI-STYLE CHAIR.

**ABOVE** MODESTLY EMBELLISHED WITH BRASS HARDWARE, THE LIVING ROOM'S SIDEBOARD IS BACKED BY AN ANTIQUE BELGIAN TAPESTRY. TO THE LEFT ARE THE COLUMNS LORRAINE FOUND IN A SALVAGE YARD.

"I don't like vivid colors," says Lorraine. "I want things peaceful and serene." With this in mind, she used a multitude of whites and creams for both walls and furnishings. She even painted the hardwood floors in the living and dining rooms white.

**RIGHT** A ROCOCO PORCELAIN CANDELABRA AND ANTIQUE SILVER TRAY WITH DEMITASSE CUPS ADD EUROPEAN FLAIR TO THE BUFFET.

**OPPOSITE** LORRAINE TURNED THE SECONDHAND RUG UPSIDE DOWN BECAUSE THIS WAY "ALL THE COLORS FADE AWAY. THEY GET VERY MUTED ON THE WRONG SIDE, AND IT GIVES THE APPEARANCE OF A NEEDLEPOINT RUG."

**PAGES 246–247** DISCOVERED IN A THRIFT SHOP, THE BREAKFAST ROOM'S LOUIS XVI-STYLE CHAIRS WERE REVIVED WITH PAINT AND UPHOLSTERY. A COAT OF WHITE PAINT UNIFIES THE TABLE, ARMOIRE, AND CHANDELIER, AND WHITE ACCESSORIES ENHANCE THE LUMINOUS EFFECT.

Hunting for furniture rich with interesting details and strong lines, Lorraine found a majority of pieces in thrift stores, junk shops, and antiques markets. Restored to new life with paint, upholstery, and fabric, the furniture reflects French and Italian influences with sensuous curves, applied trim, and lush fabrics. Gold and silver accessories and unusual architectural elements contribute to the Old World feel too. Case in point: two fiberglass columns that Lorraine rescued from a salvage yard. Cleaned up and topped with olive branches, they were positioned as an airy divider between the living and dining rooms.

(CONTINUED ON PAGE 250)

A THRIFT SHOP FIND,
THE FRENCH BED WAS
PAINTED WHITE FOR
SUBTLE CONTRAST TO
THE MOSS-COLORED
BENCH CUSHION AND
TAUPE DRAPERIES AND
CURVACEOUS CHAIR.
LORRAINE CREATED
THE AREA RUG BY
SURROUNDING A LARGE
RECTANGLE OF VELVET
WITH NEEDLEPOINT
BORDERS.

Lorraine kept the artwork to a minimum, and the few antique tapestries and rugs she allowed were faded, their colors aged to a gentle whisper. Finally, she mixed faux with real, not worrying about the "rightness" or "wrongness" of her compositions, only paying attention to what looked good.

While there are carved swags, curvy legs, lace, and cupids galore, Lorraine kept the rooms from feeling too fussy or fragile. Her design secrets? Using solid fabrics, such as the dining chair cushions of taupe velvet, and large furniture pieces with straight lines, such as the antique secretary and sideboard in the living room.

Far from its dreary beginnings, the home is now a favorite meeting spot for friends and family. Acknowledging both the couple's shared European heritage and their diverse personalities, the house is proof positive that faux opulence can be better than real simplicity.

ABOVE A GLASS TOP RESTING ON A CAST-CONCRETE BASE CREATES AN INTIMATE DINING SPOT IN THE BEDROOM.

OPPOSITE CARVED SWAGS ADD A GRACEFUL NOTE TO THE DRESSING TABLE'S STRAIGHT LEGS.

# Easy Harmony

## A FRENCH COUNTRY HOUSE HAS TOUCHES OF THE BIG CITY.

**LEFT** MAUVE TULIPS IN A GARDEN URN BRING A TOUCH OF THE OUTDOORS INTO THE DINING ROOM.

**OPPOSITE** LIKE SO MANY HOMES ON THE CÔTE D'AZUR, THE HOUSE FEATURES BRIGHTLY PAINTED DOORS AND SHUTTERS.

OPPOSITE IMBUING
THE LIVING ROOM
WITH A LIVED-IN-FOR-
GENERATIONS LOOK ARE
THE THICK WALLS AND
MASSIVE LIMESTONE
FIREPLACE. SUNFLOWERS
IN A TÔLE VASE AND
TRADITIONAL PROVINCIAL
FABRICS IN RED, BLUE,
AND YELLOW ADD TO
THE SOUTH-OF-FRANCE
MOOD.

W"We love Provençe and the French country look," says Caroline Farwell, "but we also love the formality of the northern part of the country, such as in Paris, with its moldings and elegant detailing." The house that she and husband, Tony, built in La Jolla, California, is a beautiful blend of both.

Taking nearly five years to complete with the help of architects Tony Crisafi and Drex Patterson, the residence resembles a "relaxed French manor house more than a French farmhouse," in Crisafi's view. Wrapped in stucco and topped by tiles salvaged from a farm in Bordeaux, it welcomes visitors with delphinium-blue shutters and doors and wrought-iron balconies hung with potted geraniums.

Inside, the rich wood furnishings glow in creamy, yellow-glazed rooms which, depending on their use, exhibit a variety of detailing. In the dining room picture-frame molding adds depth and dimension. "The panels break down the scale of these formal rooms so that they look and feel more intimate," explains Crisafi. The family room, which is more casual, sports rough-hewn fir beams and rafters at the 10-foot ceiling. It also features a grand limestone fireplace nearly devoid of decoration. "Because we really wanted this to be a gathering spot for our family, we built a raised hearth for the fireplace to put the flames at eye level and to provide a place to sit when the fire was low and people were clustered around," Caroline adds.

OPPOSITE THE DINING ROOM'S OAK SIDEBOARD IS A FAMILY HEIRLOOM. THE GILT CHANDELIER AND SCONCES ARE EUROPEAN IMPORTS.

Inspired by vintage French etchings, the airy kitchen exudes a decidedly provincial allure. Dark-stained ceiling beams, distressed walnut floors, and classically styled cabinets are similar to those Caroline had seen on her several fact-finding tours of France. Catering to her family of five, it was designed, she says, "to be devoted to dining and socializing." And with its shaped, granite-top island surrounded by oft-occupied rush-seated chairs, it is. (CONTINUED ON PAGE 263)

**ABOVE** CEILING BEAMS, RUSH-SEATED CHAIRS, AND A FURNITURE-LIKE ISLAND DEFINE THE FRENCH FLAVOR.

**OPPOSITE** THE KITCHEN MAINTAINS A COUNTRY AIR WITH APPLIANCES STOWED BEHIND WOOD PANELED DOORS AND DECORATIVE TOUCHES SUCH AS WHEAT ILLUSTRATION ON THE STOVE HOOD.

**PAGES 260–261** THE LARGE MASTER BATH IS FILLED WITH LIGHT FLOWING THROUGH FRENCH DOORS AND REFLECTED IN THE ENORMOUS MIRRORS. THE COUNTERTOPS ARE TRAVERTINE; THE FRENCH-STYLE FAUCETS ARE REPRODUCTION.

More Parisian in mood is the sumptuous master bedroom suite. Located on the second level, the bedroom commands a glorious outside view with two walls of windows. From the four-poster bed, the sensuously carved fireplace in the adjoining sitting room seduces the eye. In the bathroom an immense French-style tub delightfully decorated with flowering vines by a local artist takes center stage, surrounded by huge arched mirrors, crystal-dripping sconces, and lace-curtained windows that add more than a little *je ne sais quoi* to the turn-of-the-century ambience.

A distinctive blend of elements from all over France, this might be a small château, but it has a great deal of charm.

ADJOINING THE MASTER BEDROOM IS THE COUPLE'S PRIVATE SITTING ROOM. THE ARCHED CASEMENT WINDOWS AND SIMPLE CABINETRY BELOW PROVIDE THE BALANCE NEEDED FOR THE INTRICATELY CARVED FIREPLACE MANTEL.

# Pecans & Provence

## The most important accessory in this Texas house is the sun.

LEFT The mix of antique with contemporary, natural with synthetic, is an essential theme in French country decor.
OPPOSITE Bright as the morning, the entry hall is a graceful beginning to the residence the homeowner calls her "light therapy."

**OPPOSITE** A GENTLE SWEEP OF WROUGHT-IRON RAILING OUTLINES THE STAIRCASE IN THE ENTRY HALL.

**RIGHT** THE OWNER TRIED SEVEN SHADES OF OCHER FOR THE EXTERIOR BEFORE SETTLING ON THE ONE SEEN HERE.

**PAGE 268–269** NEUTRAL-TONED UPHOLSTERY DRAWS ATTENTION TO THE SILHOUETTES OF THE ELEGANT ANTIQUE FURNITURE AND CREATES AN EASY AMBIENCE IN EVEN THE MOST FORMAL ROOMS.

Like the dazzling sunlight that vibrates with energy in Van Gogh's paintings, light defines and shapes Mary Louise Sinclair's new home. Whether dappled or direct, the light dances into rooms and plays across walls, floors, and furnishings, creating a magical mood.

The goal of capturing maximum light guided the design of the house inside and out. On the front of the house, tall, shuttered windows with 20 and 24 panes recall French doors. A majestic pecan tree and a leafy pergola filter the light and soften high-summer harshness. Inside, Mary Louise arranged the floor plan to take advantage of the sun's position throughout the day. Then, with the help of interior designer Josie McCarthy, she chose a warm color palette of white, saffron yellow, terra-cotta, and muted green for fabrics and walls. The quiet shades act as a neutral background for her antiques and family pieces, adding to the importance of each. (CONTINUED ON PAGE 270)

Mary Louise's previous house was a large Tudor heavy on chintz, so this move to minimal pattern and neutral color was a radical change. And it required that she pare down the belongings she had brought from her previous home. But, she explains, "It makes you much more discriminating. You only use the things you really love."

Touches of formality, such as the leopard-cushioned, faux bamboo stool in the living room and collection of prized porcelain in the family room, exist, but for the most part the furniture is relaxed and easy. Deep sofas are strewn with a multitude of tapestry and needlepoint pillows, and guests find comfortable seating in leather bergères and chairs covered in provincial prints. "We wanted a family house that didn't have any untouchable or rarely used rooms," says Mary Louise.

OPPOSITE THE FAMILY ROOM TAKES ON A COUNTRY AIR WITH ITS MIX OF PATTERNS, EXPOSED BEAMS, AND RUSTIC ACCENTS SUCH AS THE HANDMADE CHAIR FROM THE ORKNEY ISLANDS AND GRAND-SCALE BASKET FOR FIREWOOD.

OPPOSITE MARY LOUISE GAVE THE KITCHEN A DECIDEDLY PASTORAL STYLE. THE FURNITURE IS FRUITWOOD, THE FLOORING IS TERRA-COTTA TILES, AND THE PLASTER RANGE HOOD IS DECORATED WITH PLATES FROM HER COLLECTION OF FRENCH POTTERY.

RIGHT SIMILAR TO THOSE IN A PARISIAN BISTRO, THE BANQUETTE CUSHIONS HANG FROM A BRASS ROD. THE FLORAL STRIPE OF PINK AND GREEN ADDS A FRESH TOUCH.

Walls were intentionally kept simple, highlighted only by delicately carved, white-painted millwork or, as in the dining room, adorned with subtle stripes that shimmer from the light that comes through diaphanous silk draperies. In the entry hall, a polished heart-pine floor made of wood recycled from a Mississippi flour mill exudes a soft glow. In the kitchen, tall, uncurtained casement windows allow the sun to add a gentle gleam to the glazed finish of the light green cabinetry, terra-cotta flooring, and glossy white beaded-board ceiling. And as is so common in Provence, there's a table placed in a sunny corner for family breakfasts and simple Sunday suppers.

In the master bedroom, a trumeau mirror, a beautifully worn antique carpet, and gilt candlesticks and picture frames suggest a more formal style. Even here, however, there are rough-hewn baskets and painted wood furniture to bring it down a notch.

Inspired by the south of France and exuding quiet elegance, the dwelling is so warm and inviting, says Mary Louise, "that when people step through the doors they can't believe it's a new house."

THE MASTER BEDROOM IS A HAVEN OF TRANQUILLITY. THE CREAMY PALETTE AND SIMPLE FURNITURE ARE RESTFUL ON THE EYES YET, WITH THEIR SUBTLE TEXTURES, INTERESTING, AS WELL.

# Bicoastal Beauty

AN ANTIQUES DEALER BRINGS HER FAVORITE TRADITIONS OF SOUTHERN FRANCE BACK HOME TO SOUTH CAROLINA.

**LEFT** HARMONIOUS IN THEIR DIFFERENCES, THE CLEAN-LINED FURNITURE IN THE UPPER-LEVEL SITTING ROOM IS THE PERFECT FOIL FOR THE PATTERNED CARPET.

**OPPOSITE** THE DRAMATIC, TWO-STORY FOYER SETS AN ELEGANT TONE FOR THE HOUSE WITH THE SWEEPING BALUSTRADE AND ROUND ROSEWOOD TABLE.

**OPPOSITE** POSSIBLY DATING BACK TO THE 9TH CENTURY, THE LIMESTONE MANTEL IN THE LIVING ROOM IS COMPLEMENTED BY SOLID FURNITURE WITH STRONG SILHOUETTES.

**RIGHT** EXUDING FRENCH FORMALITY WITH ITS SYMMETRICALLY PLACED WINDOWS, THE FACADE BOASTS A LIMESTONE FRONT-DOOR SURROUND FOUND AT A SALVAGE MARKET IN A REMOTE CORNER OF PROVENCE.

With an eye and ear for the lingua franca of interior design, antiques dealer Bettie Dixon had collected scores of ideas during two decades of travel between her offices in France and North Carolina. When she and her husband, Sewell, decided to build on Kiawah Island, South Carolina, they were clear, she says, that they "wanted a house that would relate primarily to the ocean while also reflecting the comfortable European homes that we had come to know."

Those homes, centuries-old structures found throughout Provence, combine French and Italian influences. The Dixons' choice of architect, Christopher Rose, couldn't have been better: He had studied and taught architecture in Genoa, Italy, and, says Sewell, "he immediately realized what we wanted." Working closely, they assembled every element of the property—from the arched portico entrance on the outside to the family heirlooms and antique treasures on the inside—to exude the style of France and the spirit of the Mediterranean.

Grand, but never too much, the exterior references *bastides*, country estates of southern France, and the 16th-century

villas of Italian architect Andrea Palladio. Shuttered casement windows and a mottled tiled roof bring the architecture back to its more pastoral roots. A loggia connecting the living room to the pool pays homage to Roman villas with their internal courtyard gardens.

New limestone flooring inlaid with antique terra-cotta tiles extends from the entrance foyer through the main-level rooms. In the dining room, heart-pine rafters salvaged from a South Carolina barn invoke the beamed ceilings of French country villas. Plaster walls tinted with pigment in soft sunlit tones warm the large-scale rooms with the texture and light one sees on the Côte d'Azur.

**OPPOSITE** THE DISTRESSED CABINETRY, MARBLE COUNTER AND BACKSPLASH, BASKETS, AND IRON CHANDELIER LEND A BEEN-THERE-FOREVER FEELING TO THE NEW KITCHEN.

**RIGHT** ADDING TO THE VARIETY OF SURFACES IS THE STONE MOSAIC INTERIOR OF THE VEGETABLE SINK.

**PAGE 284** THE CONTRAST OF LIGHT AND DARK AND THE VARIETY OF TEXTURES CREATE A RICH MOOD FOR THE BEDROOM WITH ITS 19TH-CENTURY FOUR-POSTER, WILLIAM IV MAHOGANY HIGHBOY, AND HARDWOOD FLOORS.

**PAGE 285** PROVING THAT OPPOSITES ATTRACT ARE THE MASTER BATH'S VENETIAN MIRROR ABOVE THE CONTEMPORARY BASIN PERCHED ON THE ANTIQUE BUREAU-TURNED-VANITY.

To ensure authenticity, the trio made extensive buying trips to southern France. Spending days digging through wares, they assembled some 13 tons of extraordinary treasures. Included in the containers they shipped home were the circa 9th-century limestone mantel Bettie believes to be from Normandy, now the centerpiece of the living room; the 92-inch-long 18th-century buffet around which the dining room was built; and a variety of columns, tiles, ironwork, and fragments that were used to embellish the facade and add character to interiors. Equally dazzling were such accessories as the 18th-century tapestry from Avignon and a Louis XVI trumeau selected for their majestic scale as well as their rarity and beauty.

With pool and ocean steps away, the *joie de vivre* that permeates the house extends deliciously outward. A personal vision combining the best of both worlds, this is a home for the well-lived life.

# dare to dream
## be inspired and make your dream a reality

great american
**kitchens**
collection

GREAT **KIDS' ROOMS** COLLECTION

GREAT **TRADITIONAL STYLE**

GREAT **DECKS** & OUTDOOR LIVING

GREAT **BATHS** COLLECTION

{ Style and Inspiration combine to bring you the best design ideas. Look for these inspiring titles where home improvement books are sold. }